Opening the door to the life you always wanted

From Welfare to Wealth

*A True Testimony of Faith and
The Power of Positive Thinking*

VERONICA L. REED

authorHOUSE®

AuthorHouse™
1663 Liberty Drive
Bloomington, IN 47403
www.authorhouse.com
Phone: 1-800-839-8640

Author's Note Regarding Names:
This book is based on actual events relative to the author's life. In some cases, real names have been used. However in most cases, the names have been changed in order to protect the privacy of those individuals.

First published by AuthorHouse 5/3/2010

ISBN: 978-1-4490-3128-2 (e)
ISBN: 978-1-4490-3126-8 (sc)
ISBN: 978-1-4490-3127-5 (hc)

Library of Congress Control Number: 2009912785

Printed in the United States of America
Bloomington, Indiana

This book is printed on acid-free paper.

Dedication

This book is dedicated to my parents (Mama, Daddy and Dad), without whom I could not have been here to share these thoughts with the World. Thank you for giving me life, guidance and wisdom in your own special way, so that I could help others find and realize their dreams.

To my Reed brothers: Earl Fitzgerald, Melvin Reed, Sr., Earl Reed, Jr., and Adam J.Reed. This is my gift to each of you, so that you might share my life and feel as though you were there from the very beginning!

Table of Contents

Introduction   xi

Chapter 1: My Life With Welfare…The Beginning   1

Chapter 2: 69ᵗʰ and 74ᵗʰ Streets   6

Chapter 3: Daddy's House and The Year that Changed My
Life   10

Chapter 4: Junior High School Passion and Alterations   16

      Lesson I: *Take from life those experiences that make
you a better person, because every one of us
has the ability to demonstrate goodness in
some way—our own way.*

Chapter 5: High School and Independence   25

      Lesson II: *Determination will influence your destiny.*

      Lesson III: *Dream it, believe it, and you shall see it!*

Chapter 6: Life-Changing Experiences   34

      Lesson IV: *Children are people too.*

Chapter 7: High School Passion   41

      Lesson V: *Life is truly what you make it, by what
you desire.*

      Lesson VI: *To live is to give.*

Chapter 8: Fear and Turning Points   52

Chapter 9: A Potential Roadblock   62

Chapter 10: My College Beginnings   66

Chapter 11: College and More Turning Points   72

         Lesson VII: *Optimism and Intrinsic Motivation are Keys to Success*

Chapter 12: Life Beyond College   77

         Lesson VIII: *God always places people around us to help guide us.*

Chapter 13: More College, and Then AIDS   83

         Lesson IX: *God gives us all freedom of choice and free will.*

Chapter 14: A Blessing and a Curse   87

         Lesson X: *Everything happens for a reason.*

Chapter 15: Learning How to Forgive   93

         Lesson XI: *Focus on that which is positive.*

Chapter 16: Graduate School   96

         Lesson XII: *Life is about helping and encouraging others to reach their fullest potential.*

Chapter 17: AIDS and Willpower   103

Chapter 18: Life After Someone Else's Death   108

         Lesson XIII: *Motherhood and womanhood are responsibilities that shape the future for a lifetime.*

         Lesson XIV: *"We become what we think about."* *--Earl Nightingale*

Chapter 19: Time to Move On to A New Adventure   119

         Lesson XV: *Life is about sacrifices.*

Chapter 20: The Work/Career "Life Cycle"   125

Chapter 21: Obtaining Work/Life Balance   128

Chapter 22: Deciding Which Way to Turn   133
     Lesson XVI: *Always turn to your Spiritual Maker*

Chapter 23: We Can Make Life What We Want It To Be   138
     Lesson XVII: *See yourself not as someone in need, but someone with the power to help others.*

Chapter 24: From Family Pain to Great Endeavors   149
     Lesson XVIII: *Faith is knowing that the things, which you cannot see, truly can and will exist.*

Chapter 25: For Closure and Inspiration.... Be Inspired   160
     Final Lesson: *As you share your talents with the world, the world will share its talents with you.*

Author Insights   165
     On Buying and Maintaining Real Estate   165
     On Depression   170
     On Life and the Gift of Giving   178
     About God   181

Recommended Reading and Listening   185

Appendix   187

Acknowledgments   191

Introduction

Listening to Your Inner Spirit, Your Source...God

July 10, 1971 -- a new daughter is born. For unto the world is born this day, in the City of Los Angeles, a savior in her own right who was named Veronica. No, I am *not* Jesus Christ, but I am *like* Jesus. You see we all are like Jesus because this is how God made us. He made us all as supreme beings. No matter what condition, situation, or economic level we live in, we are all like Jesus. But for a variety of reasons -- that we are sometimes unaware of -- we decide that we don't want to position ourselves as Jesus-like.

From Welfare to Wealth is not a get-rich-quick scheme. It is a story – my story. We all have a story. The best stories are not fiction – they are based on the everyday lives that many human beings have lived. *From Welfare to Wealth* happens to be my story. But it is more than that. It is a sharing of how I learned to change the way I think – of my desire to help you change the way <u>you</u> think, so you can open the door towards the life you've always wanted, as I did. *From Welfare to*

Wealth is also a blueprint… a process of building that can help you move from negative thought patterns to positive ones.

In this book I will share many experiences and situations that have occurred over the course of my life. Some of them could have caused me to stop believing in God and myself. However, I remained on course with the belief that the circumstances surrounding my experiences were only temporary. In addition, I knew that with God's help, not only would I make it successfully through, but also more often than not, I would come out on top!

Through each experience I have realized that you cannot dwell on any shortcomings in a negative manner because the more that you do this, the longer you remain stuck in that situation. Consistently speaking and thinking about that unfortunate situation in a non-positive manner will also attract more negativity into your life. But if you focus on that which you want in your life, eventually you will see it come to pass. See and think about the goodness in your life, and everything else will be well too.

It is my hope that you will have a better understanding of why it is so important to be mindful of what you say and think. Your thoughts and vocalizations tend to have a powerful impact on the outcome of every situation you are faced with, and on your life overall.

What I hope to pass on to you is the idea that not only does *your* past help you to learn and grow, but also the pasts of others with whom you may come in contact or read about. Our lives, and those of people who existed in the world before us, are lessons for each of us. However, we must have an open mind and be willing to learn from others and ourselves. You see, this is a basic premise of life that allows each one of us to move forward with confidence and success. There are mistakes that have already been made for us -- by our parents, members of our families, and even perfect strangers whom we learn about in books, real-life movies, or stories heard from those around us. We are all in a position to lead happy and productive lives, as long as we believe that we can do this and make doing it one of our goals in life.

Negative circumstances come into our lives only to teach us a lesson and make us stronger. However, ordinarily, they do not show up to create permanent pain and misery for us. This only happens if we see the circumstances as such and allow them to prevail over our lives in a negative manner. Difficult situations *must* be experienced in order for us to successfully transition into the next phase of our lives. Although we might be unaware of this at the time, hardships provide the way for greater meaning and understanding of life.

Believe it or not, without these trials, we are unable to appreciate certain aspects of life. We must endure pain in order to recognize peace and well-being. As it has been said many times before -- in the absence of opposites, balance is non-existent. Yet balance is essential to the maintenance of life. In order to embrace warmth, one must have previously experienced cold, and vice versa. Whatever the storm you are experiencing, one day it will pass and the sky will clear.

Regardless of what your current financial status is -- whether you are on welfare or extremely financially wealthy -- if you are unhappy with your life, this book is intended to help you become happy about who you are, where you are, and what you are. Happiness in life doesn't come from material possessions or status in life. Instead, it stems from feeling good about who we are on the inside, and knowing every day of our lives that we were made in God's image with His approval. Happiness is about seeing what's positive in life and focusing our energies on that goodness. We all have challenging circumstances and crap that show up in our lives, but we cannot allow the junk and the temporary negative situations to dictate our life's path.

At this point in my life, I can honestly say that what I have learned is to always stay true to God and know without any doubts that He is going to be there. How do you learn to know this without any doubt? It is something called **Faith**. And what is Faith some may ask? *My* definition of Faith is "knowing, that with God behind you it doesn't matter what lies ahead of you because His power always prevails."

Faith also involves knowing that what you cannot see truly does exist. It provides the strength to know that, even though you have a "D" average now in your sophomore year of school, by the middle of your junior year, you will have a "C" average, and by your senior year you will have a "B" average. This is real Faith in action. It is knowing that the invisible, what you cannot see, can and will come into visibility in your life. As long as you know something to be true in your heart, and you have the conviction that it is true, it will come to pass simply because you dwell upon this fact.

Anything that you desire can come to fruition through Faith, especially if what you desire is something that is meant especially for you. Napoleon Hill indicates in his book, *Think and Grow Rich*, that "faith removes limitations." As long as you have the conviction – meaning faith -- and determination to accomplish something, it shall come to pass because all obstacles are overcome by Faith.

Furthermore, faith also stems from gratitude. According to Wallace D. Wattles, author of *The Science of Getting Rich*, "Faith is born of gratitude. The grateful mind continually expects good things, and expectation becomes faith...He who has no feeling of gratitude cannot long retain a living faith."

So -- do you want positive change in your life, as well as a life that gives you ultimate bliss? If your answer is yes, then believe with all your heart, and maintain an attitude of gratitude for that which you already have. If you proceed in this manner, then peace, happiness and contentment with life will come to you.

Having said this, I need to add that there is one other requirement for obtaining inner peace and happiness. You must live your life in a manner that is pleasing to God. How can we do this?

In all of our dealings, we can determine whether they are actions that will please God. Would He smile or frown upon your action, or your decision? When in doubt, ask God and He will provide an answer for you. If you have no concept of God, or of the Supreme Intelligence that truly does exist, then I ask you to go within and ask *yourself* whether your actions will help all those that are involved or affected in some way by your actions, or whether your actions will hinder or cause harm to them in some way? If you know the difference between right and wrong, then you will know whether your answer to this question results in your proceeding with your actions, or abandoning them in order to choose a better alternative for both yourself and any others who are directly or indirectly affected by what you do.

By the time you have finished reading this book, several changes will have occurred. Your mindset will be different. You will have quite a few new tools that will take you through the remainder of your life peacefully, with thanksgiving and a knowing that with God, you are in command of your life. You will have grown to an understanding that circumstances do not control your life. Most important, you will have obtained a mental wealth called Faith, which will carry you through any tribulation that life throws upon you.

God gives guidance to each of us. But many of us -- the great majority of the human population, in fact -- decide not to take His advice and/or His direction for our lives.

My sister Peggy was a great example of this kind of decision. At our church – which was Good Tidings Baptist Church, located in Los Angeles -- many people liked her despite her peculiar attitude and demeanor. Peggy had a heart of gold, and most people knew it. She also had what could have developed into a nice, strong melodic voice. People at church, myself included, felt that she should lead more songs in the choir. Sunday after Sunday, she was encouraged to lead, but most of the time she wouldn't do it even if her life depended upon it. On the Sundays that she *did* lead songs, you'd swear someone dragged her to the microphone and forced her to stand there and sing. She never smiled, nor sang with any energy, even though her voice had all that potential.

God may not have been leading Peggy to become the next Mahalia Jackson, but at this point in her life, He did want her to bring joy to others through her voice. By "others," I don't mean the World or the Nation – I refer only to those in our church and possibly other churches whom our congregation would fellowship with. But Peggy passed up the opportunity to make a difference in the lives of these "others." No, she didn't speak proper English or look like a runway model, but she could have helped many of these church members, if only for a few minutes, through her song. But she declined God's offer.

We are all God's children, yet many of us act like rebellious children. Deep in our hearts, we know that some of our actions and words would never be pleasing to Him. Yet we do what suits us, even though it's probably not what is *best* for us.

But we can't always judge a book by its cover, so there's more to Peggy's story. There were actually quite a few reasons why my sister Peggy was who she was at this point in her life. They will be revealed later in this book.

Unlike my sister Peggy, I would (for the most part, by some miracle!) usually listen to God's lead. But -- let me be frank with you -- I didn't know it at the time. As a child I didn't realize that my decisions and actions were coming from God and that one day I would look back on my life and realize that He was the reason I made many of the choices in my life. He was the reason I was placed in certain situations and positions.

Here is one example of how that happened to me. During my senior year of high school, when I tried out for cheerleading and was selected, the school administration couldn't decide which individual to make Cheerleader Captain, so they chose three team co-captains. One of my best friends, Kathryn, and I were selected as two of the three co-captains.

One day shortly after that decision, Kathryn came to me and told me, "Veronica, I don't think the squad should have three co-captains. I feel the squad needs a leader - someone who will make final decisions. Someone who gives direction – even resolve a conflict if we need it. I want *you* to be Captain."

Kathryn assured me that she and the other girl would remain co-captains. Her reasoning was that I knew how to handle difficult situations -- that I would always make the best effort to be non-biased when making my decisions. She wouldn't allow me to say no.

"I'll be there for you whenever you might need to smack somebody," Kathryn added jokingly.

So the administration changed their decision, and I accepted the position. It turned into a very good role for me, and benefited the squad as well.

Sometimes God has a way of intervening in our lives and providing the way for us, while we labor under the illusion that the way opened up for us because of something that we ourselves are doing. Oftentimes we assume that we are in control and creating the wealth in our lives, when in actuality it is really our Divine Source that is helping us to lead more beneficial lives.

How did I eventually come to realize this important fact? It was life itself, and my observation of it, that has allowed me to understand why some people behave as they do, and why they are the persons they are today. Hopefully you will come to the same realization once you have read my story in its entirety.

I hope you will read on -- and be inspired to become the person you were destined to flourish into. If you do, you will go from a welfare mentality to a wealth mentality. You will always be at peace. You will always know that you can have, do or be anything you choose and were intended to be. And, along the way, you can aspire to be great as you help others along the way.

As Tavis Smiley says, "While you can be successful without being great, you can't be great without being successful." Enjoy!

Chapter 1

My Life With Welfare...The Beginning

In 1968, when my mother left Summit, Mississippi and migrated to Los Angeles, she had just filed for divorce and was also pregnant with her husband's last child, my sister Peggy. Since she had no husband and no job, and was merely looking for a way out of her miserable marriage and a new start on life, she applied for welfare. This is how my life with welfare began. Three years after coming to California, my mother gave birth to her 5th and final child...me. And since she was unmarried and unemployed, she was still eligible for welfare.

My experience growing up on welfare is what made me realize, even as a kid, that I wanted no part of welfare when I grew up. I can remember vividly the day in particular that made me despise welfare, and vow that I would never rely on such a system to raise my family, should I ever have one. It happened when I was in the fourth or fifth grade – a time in my life when I battled with shyness and sensitivity, especially when I had to participate in something I wasn't fond of.

That day, some of my classmates and I were selected to participate in our school chorus for the upcoming holiday program. After lunch, we were sent to the auditorium where we were under the supervision and guidance of the music teacher, Ms. McDaniel. During the music rehearsal, the remainder of our class was having a lesson on safety, which was being led by some special visitors from our local fire department. Of course my other classmates and I were going to miss this valuable safety lesson because we had to go to the auditorium for music. As irony would have it, my interests at the moment were more powerfully on safety than music.

I have no idea why I felt so strongly. But I did. So I battled with my shyness, pulled together all my courage and marched up to Ms. McDaniel. "Please," I asked her, "Can I be excused so I can go back to my class and learn about safety?"

Ms. McDaniel frowned down at me. She loved music, so she didn't appreciate nor understand my request -- and took the liberty of letting everyone in the auditorium know how she felt about it. She yelled, "You want to learn about safety instead of music? What kind of sense does that make?"

Naturally I felt shattered. Through the remainder of music class, I sat counting the minutes until I could escape and go home.

When school was dismissed, two of my best friends, La Keesha and Kathryn (who had witnessed my embarrassing moment), walked me to my mother's car with great empathy. When we got to the car, I explained to my mother, through teary eyes, the horrible experience I had just had. Unfortunately this event happened to have fallen on either the 1st or the 15th of the month, the two days that welfare checks were issued. My mother had received her check.

"I've got to go somewhere, and I'm in a hurry," she told me brusquely. "I don't have time to deal with your little music-teacher thing."

Kathryn and La Keesha looked at each other and shrugged their shoulders -- they knew that this was as far as it was going to go. My mother hurried me into the car and off we went to Bank of America's L.A. Industrial Branch on Gage Avenue and Avalon Boulevard, so she could cash her check.

That day had a tremendous impact on my life. For as long as I lived on this Earth, I would see to it that I didn't ever need to rely on welfare to take care of myself. Because at that moment, as a nine- or ten-year-old who just wanted a little reassurance that I hadn't done anything wrong to deserve Ms. McDaniel's yelling, I had been made to feel that a welfare check was more important to my mother than I was. From that day forward, the mere mention of "welfare" made me feel resentful.

Now, as I look back on that day, I am elated that it happened. This incident alone gave me the strength and determination that I would not allow any form of governmental assistance to take care of me. That moment also played a role in my desire to give my future children (should I ever have any) the attention they deserved. Not that my mother was being a bad mother – she wasn't. I understand now that she just wanted to beat the crowds to the bank, so she could make it home in a timely manner to get dinner going and complete her other motherly duties for the day.

I need to make an important point about welfare. At this particular time in American history (back in the 70's and early 80's), if you were an adult receiving welfare, your view of life was probably a bit tarnished and non-motivated. Since you were not allowed to work, be married, or have an adult male living in the home, your outlook on life was probably quite dismal at times, because your only means of receiving this minimal amount of income was through having children. The more children you had, the more income you would receive.

Considering that welfare was a form of "governmental assistance," I ask the question, "What other forms of income was welfare assisting?" Bearing in mind that "assistance" is a form of the word "assist," let's explore the meaning of this word. According to the *Merriam-Webster Online Dictionary,* the definition is "to give usually supplementary support or aid to." Supplementary means that something is added, or provided in addition to. So if welfare was considered "governmental assistance" and the mother seeking welfare could not be working, married or have any type of male provider living with her and her children, would it have been ok for this mom to have had a "female" provider in the home? All right, we won't go there, but do you see where I am going with this? According to the rules, there was no possibility that the mother could have any other income, so why then was welfare considered "government assistance"?

Was it considered to be in addition to the "food stamps" that anyone on welfare could also receive? But food stamps are not income. So a more appropriate term for welfare back then should have been "government income," because as a mother receiving it during this time, this was your job. All applicants were welcome, and encouraged to apply because, whether you were a novice mother or a professional one, all were accepted as long as you did not have any other "legal" methods of generating income to help yourself and the family you were attempting to raise.

Now if that wasn't a backwards and demoralizing system, I don't know what is! Can you understand now why I despised such a system? Hopefully you do.

However, Mama was more enterprising than many welfare mothers at that time. She utilized her free time to volunteer at our elementary school. For as far back as I can remember, my mother had served as president of the Parent-Teachers Association (PTA) at Sixty-Sixth Street Elementary school in Los Angeles, which is where all of my siblings and I attended during our elementary years. Mama was very active with both the PTA and the Advisory Council from the mid 70's to the early 80's. These were parent organizations of the Los Angeles Unified School District that allowed parents to have an active voice in their child's education. Mama did this faithfully until I graduated from Sixty-Sixth Street School in 1983.

Chapter 2

69th and 74th Streets

Fortunately, Mama did have other "unofficial" financial assistance for our family. This was provided by my father, Clark. "Daddy," as I affectionately called him, had always been there for Mama ever since she was pregnant with me. He had his own home that he owned in Los Angeles and therefore did not live with us. But he did spend many days and nights at our home.

During our earliest time in Los Angeles, Mama and I, plus my brother Charles and my three sisters—Margaret, Tanya and Peggy -- all lived in a home that Mama rented. First we lived in a duplex on 70th Street between Main Street and San Pedro Street. A few years later Mama found a bigger house to rent in a noisy neighborhood around the corner on 69th Street. That was where we lived for most of my elementary years.

The 69th Street community consisted of African-American and Hispanic families with both young and teenaged children. Most of us would spend many of our non-school hours playing with each other uproariously up and down the street. With this mixture of ages and cultures, 69th Street was always lively to say the least.

One Saturday or Sunday afternoon, my sister Peggy was chasing me in front of our house, between the street and our front yard. As I ran across the sidewalk, I collided with Derrick, a teenager who lived up the street, as he rode his ten-speed bike. Mama had to take me to the hospital with a broken leg. When we returned home, my siblings and a few of the other kids on the block all signed the cast on my leg, which I thought was very cool.

Another 69th Street incident happened at the home of the family next door to us to the west. The family consisted of the mom, her husband Wilson, and her three children. Actually her two oldest children were by previous relationships, while her youngest daughter Bradley was she and Wilson's child. Her son Thomas was the oldest, about 12 years of age. Everyone called him Tom for short. Her middle child was a daughter named Tammy, about 7 years old. Her youngest daughter, Bradley, was about 5.

Tammy and I were neighborhood friends, so sometimes we played at her house and other times at mine, running back and forth between the two houses. Tammy's house was actually a duplex -- she and her family resided in the front and her grandmother and aunts lived in the back. Her stepfather Wilson had always made me rather nervous because at times I would catch him staring at me for some reason. One day while we were playing at Tammy's home, Wilson for some reason wanted to give me a kiss on my cheek.

I don't recall whether it was Wilson or Tammy's mom that called us into the room where the two of them were sitting, but Wilson proceeded to pull me close to him in order to give me the kiss. Well, considering he wasn't my father and didn't have any relation to me, I wasn't too cool with this. So I resisted as much as possible, pulling myself as hard as I could in the opposite direction. Wilson was a tall man of about six feet, and quite muscular and fit, so my 7- or 8-year-old strength couldn't stand up to his manly power. He succeeded in landing a kiss on my cheek, and remarked to Tammy's mom that I was quite strong.

But that was the last kiss he ever got from me. After that, I remained out of dodge and never went to Tammy's house if he was at home. That incident made me very uncomfortable, and I was unsure whether he would want to continue giving me so- called "innocent" kisses on my cheek.

When incidents like this happened, or other experiences beyond my control that caused some sort of discomfort or trauma, whether for me or another person, I would become very nervous as a result. Since I don't particularly enjoy being under duress, I do whatever it takes to avoid such circumstances. You don't have to tell me twice to get out of the house if it is on fire.

What I learned from this experience was something that my husband and I tell our daughter today: "Use your own brain and do not allow others to think for you."

Once other people have the power to manipulate your life, you had better be sure that they have your best interests at heart, otherwise this type of maneuver can potentially place yourself in an unwanted or dangerous situation. Always think for yourself and utilize the experiences of others as guides, and you will do quite well in life.

If you are a child, then of course you must also rely on the direction and input of your parents. However, here again, you can use your own brain. It's risky to rely on the brains of your peers, because they don't have any more experience than you do. When in doubt, consult with an adult who has your best interest at heart, and you will be saved from having to engage in experiences which could be detrimental to you and your future.

As my readers can surely tell, 69th Street rarely had a dull moment. There was always something to stimulate the residents of our block.

Then, just before I finished 6th grade, Mama and my four siblings and I moved into Daddy's house on 74th Street, in the heart of Los Angeles. According to Mama, the owner of the house on 69th Street needed it for his daughter, who had previously been an actress, as I remember. She was now moving back into town, therefore it was necessary for us to find a new home. I don't remember exactly how the arrangements came about for us to move into Daddy's home, but that is where we headed.

74th Street was located in an area of Los Angeles that was much quieter than 69th Street, although it was less than a mile away. Located east of Avalon Blvd. and south of Florence Ave., it was one of those communities that just grow on a person. It consisted mostly of elderly households, and was very peaceful. During the time that we lived there, the feeling around the neighborhood was one of comfort. It really gave me a home-loving feeling – I wanted to stay there for as long as possible.

Chapter 3

Daddy's House and The Year that Changed My Life

Daddy's house was on a modest corner lot of about 3100 square feet. He had lived alone for a fairly long time. His only other child, George Jr., was grown and lived in Louisiana with his own wife and son. Daddy's house was therefore quite small -- much smaller than our rental home on 69th Street. He only needed enough room for himself, with one extra bedroom for guests. So the house's living space was about 800 sq. ft. with 2 bedrooms, a living room, dining room, kitchen and one bathroom.

There were now two adults and five children in this small, 2-bedroom home, which appeared to have more space in the backyard than it did inside! So Daddy had an enclosed patio added on to the back of the house, which is where my three sisters and I slept. I actually enjoyed our new room, which because of its new construction, encompassed the smell of new carpet. It had the pre-fabricated walls and ceilings found in most enclosed patios in Southern California.

I really enjoyed rainy days and nights in our new room. When there was a hard rain, it sounded as though there was a horse stampede running across the roof! This never frightened me since I knew it was just rain. I've always enjoyed being close to nature, so the sound of the thunderous rain made me feel relatively peaceful inside.

It was now 1983. We had been living with Daddy for a little while and had finally become acclimated to our new community. I was now in the sixth grade, nearing the end of my elementary-school adventure. I recall always making A's or B's on my report card (most of which were A's) throughout all of my elementary years. My play brother Maurice would always remind me and anyone else around us, that he had never known anyone to get mostly A's six years straight. Quite honestly, I never even thought of it like that. I just enjoyed school, and always put forth my best effort.

A motto that I lived by during my grade school years was that I was my own best competitor. As long as I competed against myself, that was a win-win situation for me. No one else had the same abilities, strengths, weaknesses, brainpower, genetic make-up, upbringing, parents, and anything else specific to my life! Yes, I might have sisters and a brother but they are not me, nor I them. It would be unfair to compare myself to others even in my classroom, even though my classmates were around the same age as me. Again, they are not I; they don't live with me and aren't exposed to the same circumstances as I am. So as long as I gave my best, things couldn't get any better for me.

This logic would go on helping me throughout my adult life. As long as I didn't compare myself to others, I was always content with who I was. The moment you start comparing yourself to others, you began to feel intimidated, unworthy or lacking in something. And if you act upon the comparison, you sometimes make choices that will likely not be the best decision for you. There will always be someone else in the world that is smarter, prettier, taller, more handsome, who speaks more eloquently, and so on. Not only this, but what works for someone else, may not work for you and those who may be affected by the decision. Therefore in order to prevent myself from thinking unfavorable thoughts about myself, or engaging in behaviors that would prove unbeneficial for my life, I would refrain from comparing myself to others.

A few weeks prior to our culmination day, the school administrators and 6th grade teachers had decided, that anyone who wished to make a speech during the ceremony must write their speech. The administrators would later decide on which students would get the honor of being a speaker for the big day. I can't recall whether I sincerely wanted to be one of those speakers, or if it was Mama who wanted me to do so. At any rate, I went to work on my speech. Mama wanted to hear it, so I shared it with her. Apparently she thought it needed to be changed a bit, so she included more about how important parents are. The next day, I turned in my speech.

When the principal announced the list of speakers, it was clear that I would not be one of them. Quite honestly, I was still battling shyness, so I felt relieved that I didn't have to memorize the speech. But Mama was still an active parent at my school, and she was not happy with the decision.

"The principal and I don't see eye to eye on some things," Mama grumbled to me. "That's why you weren't picked to speak."

Mama then lobbied for me to be chosen. But the principal dug in her heels, and the speaker decision stayed in place.

What a relief for me! It wasn't just a question of shyness now. I didn't want to do a speech simply because my mother wasn't happy and was in disagreement with the administrators. In any situation, it is always better to obtain honors as a result of your own diligence and efforts, not by default or because of some great turmoil that you or someone you know created got you there. Accomplishments are highly favored and create the most exhilarating internal feeling when they stem from the sweat of your own brow.

Sixth-grade culmination was in the middle of June. During the ceremony, I received several achievement awards that had come through my own hard work, so I felt quite honored. I can recall a few of my friends' parents telling Mama after the culmination ceremony, "Veronica is going to be President of the United States one day."

Those remarks made a strong indentation on my life. It's amazing how people who believe strongly in you and your abilities will give you motivation to always strive for the best in all that you do. Whether I would fulfill that expectation was unknown to me at that moment. However, just knowing that people thought that much about me to think that I would do a good job at it was enough. Even if I didn't become President, I knew that as long as I made something successful of myself by my own standards, I would be okay.

The Sunday after my culmination was June 19, which was also Father's Day. As we did every Sunday, my mother and sisters and I went to church. When we made it home that afternoon, my brother told us to keep the noise down because Clark (Daddy) was sleeping. But when Mama finally went to their room, she found that Daddy was now in his permanent sleep and would not be back to join us.

When the coroner came to check Daddy's body, they said that it appeared Daddy had died from natural causes. This was confirmed later when Mama received the autopsy results. Mama and my stepbrother (Daddy's other child, who lived in Louisiana) made Daddy's funeral arrangements.

Five days later, Daddy's funeral services were held at Angelus Funeral Home in Los Angeles. When I read the obituary, I learned that Daddy was 63 years old when he died. But the most interesting thing in the obituary was that I was listed as a stepdaughter, along with my other sisters and my brother, who was listed correctly as his stepson. Of course I didn't question Mama about why I had been included as a stepchild because I had already made it up in my mind that doing so would just create chaos. The legal name given to me at birth was Veronica Latrice Wilson, yet once I was old enough to understand, I had already known that I was definitely not a Wilson. However, Mama was sure to keep all our last names the same since this was her legal married name, and this looked favorable to the general public.

Another reason I did not wish to ask Mama why I was listed as a stepchild was because she was actually listed on the obituary as his wife, when I knew that she and Daddy had never been legally married. At this point I realized that there were a few flaws on the obituary, but it was definitely not my 11-year old place to question my 43-year old mother. She considered herself his wife through what's called "common law marriage" since she and Daddy had been together for over 11 years, I assumed. According to state law, three requirements must be met in order for a union to be considered such a marriage:

[1]* The couple must live together for a significant period of time (which is not defined in any state)

* Holding themselves out as husband and wife -- usually this entails but is not limited to using the same last name and filing a joint tax return.

---

1   Summarized from information obtained from www.expertlaw.com/library/family_law/common_law.html and www.nolo.com

* The couple had plans to be married.

Unfortunately, since California is not a state that acknowledges common-law marriages, I do not believe that Mama was legally considered as Daddy's wife. Whether Mama knew this or not is unknown to me. But one thing that I know for sure is this: according to what Mama had always told me, Daddy had promised his first wife on her deathbed that he would never marry again. And apparently he made sure that he kept his promise to her.

It was also from the obituary that I learned Daddy was a staff sergeant in the 92nd Infantry Division of the Buffalo Soldiers. They were the famous black infantry who fought in Italy during World War II. Although I don't recall Daddy ever mentioning this accomplishment (probably because he was quite humble), I'm sure that he was proud to have been such a part of American history. One thing that I am certain of, however, is that Daddy learned a great deal from serving in the military, including the war-time experience which those of us who haven't had it could never imagine.

Daddy's death really changed our lives because now Mama had to find other support for our family. We were still on welfare – but, as anyone who has ever been on welfare knows, that government "assistance" is simply not enough to support a whole family regardless of the size of the family. Thankfully, Mama was able to secure a job as the secretary of our church, which she held for many years to come.

Chapter 4

Junior High School Passion and Alterations

It was during this period of my life that several major life-changes would occur.

At the time of my birth, I was given the last name of Mama's ex-husband, so that it would look as though we were a cohesive family with one mother and one father. Indeed, Mama did the same thing for my other siblings as well, in order to maintain her dignity. Unfortunately, even though her action was appropriate for three of my siblings, since they were all children from Mama's ex-husband, it was not the case for my eldest sister or me.

Even though I did not carry Daddy's last name, Mama launched the legal journey to have my last name changed to Daddy's last name. Mama had gotten to know a Beverly Hills attorney through her aunt and uncle. Her aunt had worked for the attorney and his wife as their nanny/housekeeper. Sometime during the summer of 1983, Mama retained this attorney, who went on to win Mama's case. As a result, my name would get changed from Veronica L. Wilson to Veronica Wilson Clark (Daddy's last name). Later it was changed again, to Veronica L. Clark, which became my legal name for the remainder of my single life.

Meanwhile I was continuing to enjoy school, learning, and education as a whole.

Most of the kids from my elementary school (66th St. School) had matriculated to Mary McCleod Bethune Junior High School in Los Angeles. However, because my brother and sisters had been bussed to schools in the San Fernando Valley, my mother thought it would be a good idea if I also attended a different school outside of our immediate community. She therefore enrolled me at Mid-City Alternative Magnet School, which was for students in grades kindergarten through 12th grade.

Mama was under the impression that Mid-City Alternative was a school for gifted and talented students.

In reality, Mid-City turned out to be an open school for students who (in my opinion) had irresponsible ideas about education. Many of them didn't attend class, and the principal couldn't enforce attendance. During and between classes, kids smoked cigarettes in the bathrooms. Students were allowed to leave campus if they liked, during lunch and nutrition. No one checked to see whether they returned to campus when the breaks were over.

Since I rode the school bus to Mid-City, I was able to meet other kids who lived in scattered parts of Los Angeles. There was one girl who had the most beautiful hair I had ever seen. Every morning when she got on the bus, I would just stare at the back of her head, dreaming of the day when my hair might be as long and full as hers. I later found out that her name was Deidre.

One day I got up enough nerve to ask Deidre, "Is that your natural hair?"

"Oh no," she responded. "I have a jheri curl."

When I got home that afternoon, I asked Mama, "Can I get a jheri curl?"

Mama approved. A few weeks later, I went to a hairstylist named Barbara, who worked at a hair salon in Los Angeles where my cousin and aunt went for their own jheri curls. This treatment involves chemically treating the hair and then rolling it up for a few hours in order to get a wavy hair texture. When it was done, I was mostly happy with the result, although it wasn't anywhere near as full as Deidre's hair.

When Mama picked me up from the salon that afternoon, she kept looking at me. While we were walking to her car, she commented, "Oh, now you look more like Clark."

I thought to myself, "Now that's interesting -- why do I have to look more like Daddy?" Whether I looked like him or not shouldn't matter since we all knew that he was my father. I guess Mama felt that, should I ever need to attend court with her to prove that I was definitely Daddy's daughter, at least I resembled him more since Daddy, being a Creole, had wavy hair. As time passed on I would think about Mama's comment less and less, but it always remained in the back of my mind.

Although Mid-City included all grade levels, it was a relatively small school with around 400 students. It operated on the premise that kids acquired knowledge best through applied learning techniques and exposure, within small-size learning environments. In order to encourage cohesiveness, the students addressed teachers and staff members by their first names. One of the classes that I had signed up for was a cultural-perspective class where we traveled to such notable local spots as the La Brea Tar Pits, Placerita Canyon Nature Preserve, and Famous Amos Cookie Factory. This was my second favorite class after English.

English class was my favorite, however -- mainly because of the teacher, Pat, as we affectionately called him. He was an awesome teacher with a great passion for both learning and teaching. His enthusiasm was not however appreciated by most of his students. On a typical day, while Pat was graciously giving us students his all, you would find his class in chaos. Students would be walking in and out, going to and from the restroom, eating in class, and/or having sidebar conversations. There wasn't the slightest bit of attention to Pat's energy and dedication.

But it was in Pat's class that I read the novel *Lord of the Flies*. This book changed my life and perspective on survival -- it gave me a glimpse of how ordinary people, even children, can become savages when they feel that there are no boundaries.

Pat's influence also inspired me to demonstrate my creative talents in a local art contest connected to the U.S. Olympics. With Pat's encouragement, I did a drawing that depicted a hand holding a torch, with the flames blowing in the wind and some other details that I can't recall. This piece of art went on to a state art contest. By the time the winners were to be selected, however, it was the second semester of my 7th grade school year, and my mother and I had decided that I should transfer to Bethune Junior High where my other fellow classmates from my elementary school were attending, which was also much closer to our house. It was an exciting moment -- I was finally re-united with several of my friends and acquaintances from elementary school. Since I had been identified as a gifted child, I was enrolled in all magnet classes.

One day, less than a month after I got to Bethune, I was called out of class to meet with the Principal, Ms. Peggy Selma. Ms. Selma was someone whom I came to genuinely respect and admire. She always wore professional attire, and carried herself in a dignified manner.

When I went down to Ms. Selma's office, she told me, "Veronica, you won the art contest that you entered at Mid-City. You're invited to attend a luncheon with me in honor of all the winners."

Man, talk about pure shock! I couldn't believe it. My picture had actually won. Although extremely happy, I was also saddened that I couldn't share this moment with Pat, who had inspired me to just go for it. Nevertheless, I knew that he was aware that I had won -- he was one of the first to be contacted since he was my teacher at the time. Knowing this, I was reassured that he knew the effect in which his positive spirit and enthusiasm had made on at least one life in that chaotic classroom. He had helped me to do something that I probably would have never pursued prior to enrolling in his class. Through his encouragement and guidance, I not only achieved something, but also excelled in the process. I could always reach for the stars, regardless of what was going on around me. Thank you, Pat!

My first year at Bethune Junior High, I managed to maintain a 4.0 grade point average (gpa). Miraculously I achieved the same level the second year and also my third year, which earned me the honor of being school valedictorian of the class of 1986. As valedictorian, I would deliver a speech at our culmination ceremony, which would be held at an auditorium at Trade Tech College in downtown Los Angeles. I had the option of either putting my speech on note cards or doing it completely from memory. I chose the latter option because

I had gotten accustomed to doing this as a young speaker at my church, which was still Good Tidings Baptist Church.

For years already, at Easter and Christmas, I had participated in special Sunday School programs. Youth members and non-members of the church delivered all the speeches and holiday songs. Any children whose parents wanted them to participate could do so. The only requirements were that each child had to attend rehearsals, recite the speech completely from memory, and sing the designated songs with all the other children.

Participating in these church programs had launched my training as a public speaker. Considering that my mother had attended this church for as long as I can remember, I believe I must have been saying speeches ever since I was quite young. I recall always being given the longest speech for my age group, which didn't bother me since I actually enjoyed the challenge of having to memorize the speech and then impress the congregation with my execution. Since we attended church and Sunday School every Sunday, I would usually also deliver the review for my Sunday School class. The more I delivered these reviews, the more I wanted to do them – in fact I was often expected to do so if no one else volunteered.

As I had approached the pre-teenage years, I was also selected to fill in for our church announcement clerk, if she was absent during the regular 11:00 am church service. Sometimes, without any prior notice, I was called upon to say a short welcome to visitors after the announcements. I would have to make up whatever I was going to say within the few seconds it took to walk the fifteen feet from my seat to the church podium. Ultimately the job of acting as the designated church welcome committee had become my responsibility, whether the announcement clerk was present or not.

From there I had gone on to be selected president of our church's youth usher board. It was my job to facilitate our short meetings, which typically took place once a month on a designated Saturday morning. My duties also included coordinating with our usher board chairperson about any outings or activities for the group. These activities ranged from fundraisers to fun activities such as an outing at the park, trips to the local skating rink, or fellowship activities with youth usher boards from other Baptist churches.

After I had entered junior high school, my church formed a new organization for the young to middle-aged ladies. The name of this organization was The Young Matrons. Its purpose was to help the younger ladies have mentors in whom they could confide when they had questions about the Bible or any other life matter. The Young Matrons met once a week in the evening. My involvement with this group helped me to learn more about certain aspects of life as a female, relative to the impact of marriage, single parenting and other important factors of life. Not that I would ask questions about the aforementioned points. Instead I would just listen and observe. When a group of women get together, discussion of their personal lives is inevitable. As long as I had eyes and ears, I was always learning. And learning didn't have to occur in a formal educational setting either.

As you can probably tell, by the time I was selected as valedictorian of my junior high school graduating class, I had acquired quite a bit of exposure to public speaking! Now it was time to do so in front of all my classmates, parents, teachers, school administrators, and anyone else at the culmination ceremony. Fear and excitement were my emotional pals from the time I wrote my speech, until the day of the ceremony.

As I sat on the stage waiting to be called to the podium, I was still very nervous.

But surprisingly, as soon as I stood at the microphone and began speaking, the fear began to fade. Since I had written the entire speech myself, I felt proud to stand there making statements which came straight from my heart. I meant every word, which was apparently conveyed in my elocution.

Several times during the speech, the crowd erupted in applause. My excitement intensified – I knew that the crowd was identifying with what I was saying, so I couldn't wait to give them more -- everything I had, in fact. It was no longer a question of my just making it through two and a half pages of words that I had memorized. It was my duty to help the now-captivated listeners, children and adults alike, so they could leave this ceremony with words that might have a lasting impression on their lives.

Moments like this one are life changing, for both the giver and the receiver, which is truly what living is all about. During those times that allow us the opportunity to change the life of another person in a positive manner, we should more often than not be eager and willing to do so. Every one of us has the ability to demonstrate goodness in some way—our own way. Life presents us with many chances to carry out these acts of virtue. However, we must also have the courage and desire to do so.

Lesson I: *Take from life those experiences that make you a better person, because every one of us has the ability to demonstrate goodness in some way—our own way.*

You never know the impact that you can make on someone's life….especially a child's life. Back when Pat was helping me with my art contest, I'm not sure if he knew he was helping to shape a life.

It was not only his assisting me, but also his passion for his craft that sifted through to me, that pushed me to attempt something which I previously wouldn't have. For Pat to do this for me despite the disruptions in his classroom, demonstrated to me that, whatever your endeavor in this life, it has to be done with passion.

Although I had spent only one semester at Mid-City Alternative Magnet, and the school was so engulfed in chaos, it was a life-changing experience for me. My moments with Pat, as well as the field trip that my other class took to Placerita Canyon, left a mark on my life that cannot be erased. While at Placerita Canyon, I was able to just enjoy nature…the streams, beautiful trees and peacefulness that I just couldn't find in the city. So I learned to take from life those few experiences that make you a better person and those that allow you to be more grateful for the simple things in life. If it makes you smile, hold on to it for a while.

Chapter 5

High School and Independence

Lesson II: *Determination will influence your destiny.*

By the time I was in the tenth grade at John C. Fremont High School in Los Angeles, Mama had to provide only for me because all of my siblings were now over 18. At this point we were no longer getting welfare because the welfare office somehow found out about Mama's job at our church. So once again it was hard to make ends meet. However, being the determined woman that she was, Mama didn't let that hinder her. She eventually got a job as a pre-school teacher at a private Christian school in Lynwood, California.

I was now 15. Since I was painfully aware of Mama's precarious financial situation, I knew it was time for me to get employment.

An opportunity arose at Bank of America. The mother of one of my best friends, La Keesha, worked there, so she and I were able to get a permit to work. We both wanted to work in order to have our own money. For me, however, it was a way to provide for the things that I needed in high school, such as purchasing my drill- team uniform and later my cheerleading uniform during junior and senior years. Not to mention the small but important things like going to the hair salon. As an African-American female teenager in the heart of LA, you had to look attractive or be mocked and scorned for life. As for La Keesha, the job most likely would provide extra money for her to spend somewhat as she pleased, which was quite opposite of my situation.

A few positions were available at Bank of America. We had to interview with the Manager of the Statement Preparation Department at what was then called the LA Data Center. La Keesha and I both applied for the open positions, and the arrangements were made for our individual interviews. Unfortunately I missed my initial interview that had been scheduled for one afternoon. On that particular day, I had gone shopping for clothes in the morning with my boyfriend, his sister and nephew. Because we had to rely on public transportation and hadn't planned our return time efficiently, I couldn't make it to the interview.

Understandably, my mother was furious! "Look at you," she scolded me. "Out with your boyfriend and not taking care of important business!"

Feeling embarrassed, I called La Keesha's mom to see if there was any way my interview could get rescheduled. To my amazement and relief, the manager was very understanding. There was no way that I was going to miss the next interview -- Mama and I would see to that. When the day came, I arrived early, and told the manager, "I really appreciate your willingness to reschedule. If you hire me, and give me the opportunity, I will do everything in my power to not let you down."

"When can you start?" she asked.

This incident and experience is what gave me the philosophy that what is meant for you, will be yours. If you strongly desire something, and God intends for you to have it, this is what shall be done. Nothing and no one can ever take away what God has set-aside especially for you. Incidents may come and circumstances may arise, but thank God almighty, that if you keep your eyes on the prize, all that is meant for you will arrive!

Lesson III: *Dream it, believe it, and you shall see it!*

It was during our 10th grade year. Since La Keesha and I now had jobs and desperately needed at least one car between the two of us, I got a bright idea. I was an avid *Wheel of Fortune* fan. Each year I would watch the teenagers compete during *Wheel of Fortune's* annual "Teen Week" competition and dreamed of being a contestant on the show. But this year I dreamed of winning a car!

One day I decided to find out how I could become a contestant. I called the telephone number that the TV screen ran after each show. When I called, I was given the date, time and place of their next auditions. Talk about excitement! I was totally flabbergasted because I was actually going to have an opportunity to allow my dream to come true.

I just had to tell La Keesha, since she and I both wanted a car badly. After I told my mom, it was agreed that my aunt would drive us down to the auditions, which were in Hollywood, if I recall correctly. La Keesha and I both made it through the first round of auditions, but unfortunately during the second round, La Keesha was eliminated. I made it through all rounds and was chosen as a contestant. All too soon, it was show time!

That day, my mom and my sister Tanya drove me to Burbank where the show was being taped. The excitement was building! I was actually going to be on the *Wheel of Fortune* show! We arrived at the studio and were checked in. My mom and my sister were directed to the entrance for the audience, while I was led to a room where I would meet up with other contestants. There we also met Pat Sajak and Vanna White, who were both just as cordial and nice as they appeared to be on television.

The moment had arrived for my first round. By God's grace I managed to be the big winner for the day, so I went on to the bonus round. I will never forget that moment. I was standing there with Pat Sajak after I had voiced the letters that I thought would be in the puzzle. Vanna turned all the letters that I was going to get for my final puzzle. There were only a few letters illuminated, but again because of God's grace, I figured out the puzzle.

"Tax collector!" I blurted.

To my amazement that was it! I had won a 5-day trip to Hawaii. However, during that time, which was back in 1987-1988, you couldn't keep the money that you won. Instead you had to go shopping on the show and buy prizes. After winning one of the earlier rounds, I bought a 7-day trip to Australia. Those exhilarating moments were truly surreal.

Also during that time on *Wheel of Fortune* for Teen Week, the three biggest winners for that week would come back and compete on Friday, for a chance to win the car. Amazingly enough, I was one of the three.

On Friday's show, the big day of the week, the money that you won would earn you savings bonds for college. I managed to win one round for a total of $3,000 in savings bonds. At one heart-stopping moment, I came quite close to being the big winner of the day. But

I couldn't figure out that last puzzle. To this very day, I will always remember the answer, which was "High School Diploma." Strangely enough, I kept thinking it had something to do with high-school sports (maybe because I was a cheerleader!) so I kept trying to relate it to football and other athletic activities. I knew it was High School something! So I missed my chance to be in the bonus round for the car, which was my sole purpose for being there!

But I was still very humbled and thankful for the college money I had won. By no means did I regret for not being able to win the car. I did however beat myself over the head for not being able to figure out that darn puzzle. This memory is right up there with the time, during elementary school, when I misspelled the word "pedestrian" at our District Spelling Bee. Every time I see that word, I reminisce back to that day, on the stage at Bret Harte Junior High, when I spelled pedestrian "p-e-d-e-s-t-r-i-e-n." At least I think that's how I spelled it since the judges said it was wrong and I thought I had spelled it correctly with an "a." Interestingly enough, one of the teachers from my elementary school also seemed to have heard me spell it with an "a." After the competition was over he walked over and spoke with the judges to find out why it was considered incorrect. In either case, both of these moments I can recall as if they occurred last week, because I was disappointed with myself, even if only for a few moments.

My experience on *Wheel of Fortune* was memorable for other reasons than meeting Pat Sajak and Vanna White. Since I was competing with other kids in my age group, I got a chance to meet students from various parts of the country. This is how I became pen pals with a girl named Amy. Amy and I actually wrote to one another for maybe about a year. She wanted me to come visit her in Chicago, but my mom would never agree to it because she said we didn't know their family that well. Mama's reluctance was quite understandable. Our letters soon became few and far between until eventually Amy and I lost contact. But still, it was a memorable experience to meet a perfect stranger for one day out of your life, and spend the next year of your life in constant communication with them. Now that's the type of stuff that truly makes the World go around.

Another teen contestant I had met was a young African-American gentleman who also lived in Los Angeles. Unfortunately his name escapes me now, but it was he who gave me an idea. He had shared with me that, if he won a trip, he was going to offer one of the tickets (since on Teen Week all of the trips included a total of 4 tickets) to his aunt for a reasonable price, which would allow him to have some money to put in the bank. When he told me that, I felt as though this was a brilliant idea. I decided to do the identical thing for my trip to Australia once the time arose to select who would accompany me. Since I had up to a year to actually take the trip, I would not revisit the topic until the following spring.

I was now in my junior year. This particular year would turn out to be quite momentous for me.

I was just old enough to drive and get my driver's license. On April 1 of that year, I happily got my Interim Driver's License. Since I hadn't won the car, La Keesha and I still had to catch the local street bus to work during the 4 days per month that we were allowed to work due to our age. We realized that it would sure make things a lot easier for us if we had our own cars. At the moment, it would sometimes get pretty inconvenient for our parents, considering the fact that we worked after school for 4 hours each of the 4 days, and didn't get off work until 10 pm. At least one of our parents always had to pick us up from Downtown Los Angeles, which was about 8 miles from my house and approximately 14 miles from La Keesha's house. At the time, her parents were renting in an unincorporated area of Compton, California, currently known as Rosewood.

La Keesha was lucky to have a working mom and dad who either assisted her in buying her first car or bought the car outright for her. It was a used 1974 Volkswagen Bug. Although I wanted a car of my own, I knew that I couldn't dare ask Mama to help me buy a car. And I most definitely would not ask her to purchase a car for me! She wasn't able to do this for my other siblings either. It was money she just didn't have.

At the start of the summer prior to my junior year, I unashamedly decided that I would get a 2nd job over the summer. Since I only worked at Bank of America for 4 hours a day (during the school year it was 4 hours per day, 4 days a month only), there was ample room for additional employment. I was able to get a summer job through the Summer Youth Employment Program (S.Y.E.P.) sponsored by local government. There I worked in the Workers Compensation Department, filing papers from 8 a.m. to 12 noon. On days that I had to work at Bank of America, I would leave my job at Workers Comp and catch the street bus to the bank (fortunately for me, they were both located in Downtown Los Angeles), and would then work from around 12:30-4:30 p.m.

Once at Bank of America I would join up with La Keesha. After work during the summer months, before we had our cars, we would take the street bus from Bank of America to our school, Fremont High School, for cheerleading practice. Sometimes we would be a few minutes late depending on the time we were able to leave work, in addition to how timely the public buses were for that route.

Taking the bus for that period of time was motivation enough for me to save my money and buy my first car. Finally the magic moment came. Since Daddy had died, I didn't have a local male

31

figure I could rely on for automobile wisdom -- my favorite uncle (whom we affectionately called Uncle Herbert) lived in New Orleans so he was unable to accompany me. In addition, I didn't know how to drive a manual transmission at the time. So La Keesha's mom and Dad drove me to Hollywood to test-drive a car that I had found in the newspaper. La Keesha's Dad drove it for me and assured me that it ran rather well. Hearing this, I bought my first car, a yellow 1973 Volkswagen Bug from a private owner for $400.

Then La Keesha's Dad had to drive it home for me. In order for us to learn to drive a manual transmission, La Keesha's parents took the two of us to the parking lot of The Forum, located in Inglewood, early on Saturday mornings. La Keesha's car was in the shop at the time, so she learned in her mom's car, which was a current model Chevrolet Spectrum, while I learned in my car. On some Saturdays, when it was only La Keesha's mom giving us lessons, we both would take turns in her Spectrum. Needless to say, I learned how to drive that little yellow Bug, slowly but surely!

Since the prior owner had driven my Bug from Kansas to Los Angeles, it was a little rusty in some places and needed a paint job. My boyfriend at the time had a cousin who did auto-body work. I took it right over to him for an estimate and then saved the money to get the gold color I had selected, which I absolutely adored once it was on the car. This little Bug would eventually take me through the remainder of my high school years, never to let me down.

By the end of spring, more personal landmarks were coming towards me. Towards the end of April, I was also invited to a luncheon and special program, in recognition of those students who had made the honor roll. Thirteen other juniors at my school, and myself, would get inducted into the National Honor Society for having achieved significant academic standing throughout the school year. During the school day, a special ceremony was held, during which all of the students were presented with certificates and membership cards to this special organization.

A little later I also learned that a few of my other classmates and I were now Life Members and Gold Seal Bearers of the California Scholarship Federation. This honor was awarded to those students who consistently maintained a grade point average of 3.6-4.0 for at least five semesters.

At this point, a real sense of pride and acknowledgment overcame me – a realization that hard work does pay off. These accomplishments made an intense impression on my life, assuring me that you can truly do whatever you set your mind on doing. The only person, who truly has the ability to prevent you from fulfilling your goals and desires, will always be you. Yes, obstacles may come, but with determination and tenacity you will indeed prevail.

Chapter 6

Life-Changing Experiences

It was time to decide whom I would take on my trip to Australia. In my heart I really wanted one of my best friends, La Keesha, to go with me. After all, she was the one who went to the audition with me, and we had assured each other that if one of us were to win a trip, we would definitely take the other person. However, I did not know how taking La Keesha would affect my other best friend, Kathryn, so I wound up inviting my cousin Elaine. What's a girl to do!

The trip package contained round-trip tickets and hotel accommodations for four people: myself, Elaine, Mama, and one other person. Since there was one space left, I told Mama about how the aunt of the young man whom I had met at *Wheel of Fortune* had paid him so she could go. My mother went and talked to her boyfriend, Bob, then got back to me.

"Bob wants to go," she said, "and he has agreed to pay you for the fourth ticket." This was fine with me.

The trip was scheduled for the summer of 1988, and I would be a high school senior in the fall. This would be the year that I also accepted the honor of being cheerleader captain for our cheerleading squad at school. Unfortunately, as it turned out, cheerleading camp was going to be held the same week, so I wasn't going to be able to attend. Since my trip was already booked, there was no way to reschedule for risk of possibly forfeiting the trip altogether. Fortunately, since one of the co-captains on the squad was one of my best friends, she thankfully understood.

"Don't you worry," she said. "The other co-captain and I will lead the squad."

Though I was reassured in knowing that camp would go well, I was also quite torn. Cheerleading camp was something I had looked forward to for two years, ever since I first became a cheerleader. It would be a memorable experience to share with my two best friends and the other girls on the squad. In years to come, we could all look back and reminisce about the various triumphs and pitfalls we endured at camp. Well, regrettably I wasn't going to share in that little part of our high school cheerleading history. Instead, I would have to heartily accept going to not just a different country, but also a whole new continent! Wow, now that's an extraordinary option for a 17-year-old girl from the inner city of Los Angeles. It was also the opportunity of a lifetime, which I knew couldn't be surpassed.

In August, the four of us were off to Sydney, Australia. Our 13-hour flight wasn't too bad, except for being in close proximity to a young man (possibly in the age range of 16-18 years) who got airsick during the flight. Now that wasn't too pleasurable. Nonetheless, considering having to be airborne for that length of time, I had no complaints and felt totally empathetic for the guy.

From the Sydney Airport, we went straight to our hotel, which was supposedly the same hotel where Michael Jackson would stay whenever he came to the land of koalas and the home of the world-renowned Sydney Opera House. As we approached the hotel, the two well-dressed young doormen standing at the front entrance impressed us, something I had only seen on television. I was more accustomed to the Best Western Motels where Daddy and our family had always stayed during our annual summer drives from California to Mississippi.

As we approached the entrance, the doormen greeted us with smiles as they welcomed us into the hotel. Elaine and I traded eager grins after we passed the doormen, one of which was quite attractive.

Elaine and I shared a room, while Mama and Bob had their own room. Once we made it to our room, Elaine and I embraced the ambiance as we toured our hotel suite. Inside the bathroom were these beautiful brass fixtures, unlike anything we had ever seen in our young, inexperienced lives.

"This hotel is definitely top of the line!" Elaine said.

After we finished soaking up the beauty of our hotel, we all decided to go to the pier area and grab a bite to eat, then catch a sightseeing cruise. Purchasing food and splurging on activities was not a concern since my trip package also included $500 cash for spending money. Since Elaine and I weren't very hungry, we chose to grab some fries.

"Can we have some ketchup with our fries?" we asked the female cashier.

The young lady looked puzzled. After we asked a second time, she turned to her fellow cashiers hoping that someone knew what we were asking for. One of the other cashiers stepped forward and asked politely, "Do you need tomato sauce?"

Elaine and I laughed at our little blunder. Here we were thinking that the cashiers were clueless, when in reality we were the ones out of our league. It was a memorable moment.

After we had finished eating, we boarded a small cruise ship. Once everyone had secured their seats, we drifted along the Sydney Harbor where we had the pleasure of viewing many attractive hillside homes, the Opera House and various other picturesque sites. The views were absolutely stunning, especially to my mom and me, who were visiting from the inner core of Los Angeles, and my cousin Elaine, who was from Compton. As for Bob, he lived in a nicer part of L.A., so I wasn't sure whether he was seeing these types of landscapes for the first time or not.

Bob was a postman for the United States Postal Service. My understanding was that he was previously married and had two sons who were probably slightly older than I was, although I wasn't certain of those facts. Bob was about 6 feet tall and weighed between 225 to 275 pounds. He was always cordial to my sister Peggy and me, as we always seemed to be the only two around when he would come to visit. At one point Mama had told us that he wanted to marry her. But I immediately protested, stating that he could never replace Daddy. I'm not sure whether Mama had decided to honor my wishes or whether the relationship just never escalated further -- but marriage was not mentioned again.

In hindsight, I wish I hadn't spoke against Mama marrying Bob because he may have been decent companionship for her, especially once I had graduated from high school and went off to college. Hindsight is always 20/20 while foresight is usually somewhere around a -4.75, which is closer to my current actual eyesight!

As our trip progressed, we continued having wonderful mind-opening adventures. From our excursion to the Sydney Zoo, where we were able to wander amongst the koalas and kangaroos, all the way to our tour of the Opera House, we weren't ever disappointed. By the time the 7th day had come we were all pretty tired and ready to return home. Although Elaine looked like she was having a good time, there were frequent periods when she seemed to be having stomach pains which made her want to just lie down and relax. When these episodes occurred we would just retreat to our room and enjoy the lavish ambiance.

Lesson IV: *Children are people too.*

With our trip ending, we traveled to the Sydney Airport for our return flight home. As our plane departed, I sat back in my airline seat and reminisced about our weeklong excursion. I felt truly blessed and fortunate to have shared in this experience.

But a few weeks after we arrived home, I realized that Mama had not mentioned when Bob would give me the money for his ticket, as we had previously agreed. I finally found the courage to ask her when he planned to pay me. Mama politely responded, "Oh, well, he really was like our protection, so let's just leave it at that."

When I heard this, I was deeply disappointed. After that, it was hard to even look at Bob whenever he came over, knowing that a deal was a deal and he honestly should have paid me for that ticket. Although in all honesty, in Bob's defense, I'm not sure whether he even knew about the agreement or not. Did Mama even tell him that I was "selling" the extra ticket? This, I do not know. Therefore I cannot fault Bob for something he may not have been privy to.

Eventually however, I got over it and realized that I was just a child and sometimes even our own parents will take advantage of us. I honestly would have appreciated Mama just telling me from the beginning that this is how she viewed the situation. At least this way I wouldn't have been anticipating payment, especially since I was funding my own high-school activities. Every little bit counts. However, I knew that this particular little incident was not going to make or break me.

This was a learning experience for me at the time, about how to be honest with my own children once I was a parent. As much as possible, I would do my best to treat them with a sense of respect that tells them, even if subliminally, that their opinion and feelings do matter.

Once school was back in session and the year progressed, I learned the reason for my cousin's stomach pains. Pregnancy! Apparently my cousin was pregnant when we went on our trip, unbeknownst to anyone, including her mother—my aunt. Talk about a shocker! I hadn't even considered this as a possibility, especially since we were only 17. Elaine was able to conceal her pregnancy until she was about 6 months along.

In December, Elaine gave birth to her first son, Kevin, who has grown to be a handsome and bright young man.

From Elaine's experience and my experience of being jilted out of the agreed-on payment, it is my advice to all parents to take time to listen, pay attention to, and respect your children. Whether your child is self-sufficient and a joy to have around, or irresponsible and a pain in the rear, please see to it that you hear their voice. That voice could be loud and clear, or very subtle and shy, in need of fine-tuning for clarity. Whatever the case, please be sure that it is heard. Children are people too. The more that we as adults and parents are in tune with our children, the bigger and brighter the future will be -- for them, their parents and the world in general. As long as children feel that the people they care about the most are hearing their voices, they will have an inner sense of fulfillment that will take them very far in life in a favorable way. Let's not deprive them of this promising journey.

Chapter 7

High School Passion

Lesson V: *Life is truly what you make it, by what you desire.*

One of the keys to a successful life is believing. Whatever you believe is what will come to pass. If you believe you are poor, then you will always remain poor. If you believe you're a failure, you will continue to fail. If you believe that your life is going nowhere, your life will continue to be at a standstill. As Dr. Wayne Dyers says "Change the way you look at things, and the things you look at will change."

Because I had maintained a 4.0 GPA for my entire three years in junior high school, I set a goal to strive for similar results once I entered high school. I thought to myself, "If I did it once, I can do it again." After my freshman year, when I had successfully accomplished maintaining a 4.0 gpa, even while working 4 days each month during my second semester of 10th grade, actively participating in the school drill team and my church activities, I realized that this goal was definitely attainable.

During my senior year, a few more goals came along. One was to hold an appropriate position on our school's Student Council, and to be voted Homecoming Queen. Earlier in the school year, my friends and I had all agreed on who would run for which positions and honors during the year, so that we wouldn't run against each other and would have everyone's full support. For our Student Council, both La Keesha and I decided to run for the positions of Assistant Commissioner of Publicity since there were two of those positions available, and a high likelihood that we would win with minimal to no competition. We also agreed that I would run for Homecoming Queen, even though the odds were high that I would be defeated.

Over the years, the cultural dynamics of our local community were moderately changing. The Hispanic population was rapidly increasing, while the African-American population was decreasing. Many families we knew were choosing to re-locate to some of the newer suburbs just outside of Los Angeles County, such as Pomona, Ontario and Rancho Cucamonga, which are within San Bernardino County. They would also relocate to areas within Riverside County, located on the outskirts of Los Angeles County, approximately one hour away. So, by the time that I was a senior at Fremont High in Los Angeles, African-Americans were in the minority, while Hispanics held the majority of the student population, with a ratio of roughly 40% to 60%.

During this time at Fremont, race relations were quite decent, so there was very little tension amongst Hispanics and African-Americans, which was greatly appreciated by most of the students. We were really like one big "Pathfinder" (Fremont's mascot) family, which makes a huge difference in high school. When the Student

Council elections were held, La Keesha and I were voted in as Assistant Commissioners of Publicity. However, when the time came for the Homecoming campaign and elections, most of the African-Americans were quite pessimistic about the outcome. We knew that we were outnumbered, especially considering how supportive most Hispanics tend to be of one another. However, because my friends consisted of both African-Americans and Hispanics, there was a ray of hope for a successful campaign.

The day finally came for the announcement of finalists for the Homecoming Court. That day, we were all on pins and needles as we sat in homeroom (the class you had to attend daily in order to have your attendance recorded, and also where other administrative functions were handled) waiting for the names to be read. As protocol would have it, the first names to be announced were the three female finalists for Homecoming Queen.

The announcer was Mr. Gooding, one of our School Administrator's and Student Council Advisor/Chairperson. He was a guy whom we all just adored. "The names will be in alphabetical order.", he stated.

All of us sat tensely silent. There was a long beat. Then.... "Felicity Calloway," Mr. Gooding said.

We applauded. She was another African-American girl, fellow classmate and cheerleader.

Mr. Gooding paused, to build the suspense even higher. My heart was beating so fast, I thought it might jump out of its cavity. As soon as he said "Veronica" our classroom erupted in cheers.

Man, talk about excited! I don't remember whether we heard the third name because we were just thrilled that both Felicity and I had made it as finalists, and there was no one else from our class that was in the running. I just couldn't believe it. We did learn that the third finalist was Rebecca Lopez. Of course now, the real suspense would begin.

Although we were all thoroughly excited, our pessimisms still hadn't diminished, especially since we knew that the majority of African-American votes were split between Felicity and I. But one afternoon while in our Student Council class meeting, we were discussing the Homecoming results and expressing what our feelings were on what we thought the final outcome would be. Mr. Gooding was listening to our discussion.

"Don't be so sure," he calmly and nonchalantly commented. "You never know."

Upon hearing this I sat in my seat and looked at Mr. Gooding. He just went on working as if he didn't have a care in the world. At that moment, after carefully observing Mr. Gooding's mannerisms, my pessimism carefully turned to optimism. Although I didn't want to get my hopes up, there was just something about his vibe that gave me a ray of hope.

Homecoming Day was filled with various tasks that needed to get accomplished to ensure the day's success. In the morning, the first item on the schedule was making it promptly to the appointment with my hairstylist. I was worried about being late for other appointments. Kenney, my hairstylist at the time, was extremely talented and the best I had ever had up to this point in my life. However, he was always running late due to his perfectionist style, love for his work and loquacious character. Fortunately though, I was one of his first clients for the day, and managed to escape in a timely fashion.

The second item of the day sped up my heart rate a bit, because I was hoping that my escort would show up on time. Fortunately, Fremont's rules allowed non-Fremont students to participate as escorts. This was music to my ears, since Jeremy, my boyfriend at the time, did not attend Fremont. He was one year my junior, and was attending Verbum-Dei High School, which was a Catholic all-boy school located in the heart of Los Angeles in an area more commonly known as Watts. (Watts is infamous for the Watts Riots that took place during the summer of 1965, and was at the helm of the racially-stimulated uprisings of the 1960's.) But Jeremy arrived at our agreed-upon time (his parents were both punctual and trustworthy). So the remainder of the day just continued falling into place.

The gown that I wore was a sleeveless, red and white carriage dress that I was fortunate to have borrowed from a friend of La Keesha's mother. We figured red and white would be appropriate considering Fremont's school colors were cardinal red and gray. To complement my gown, Jeremy wore a white tuxedo with tails, red tie and cummerbund, and white shoes. He looked rather handsome; especially since this was the first time I had seen him in a tuxedo. I must admit that all men, regardless of what each one looks like, tend to look attractive in white tuxedos! For Jeremy, however, the tuxedo was just an added enhancement. He had really smooth skin of a brown hue, and he always had his naturally wavy hair cut just long enough to curl over once, which brought out the sparkle in his brown eyes.

After all the Homecoming Court participants arrived, we lined up along the track outside the school's football field. Special cars had been brought in so we could parade around the track. The cheerleaders brought up the rear of the parade as they rode on the fire truck with members from the local fire department. The parade was a long-time tradition at Fremont and was something that everyone looked forward to.

Then it was the moment of truth. Mr. Gooding's voice echoed around the football field – the name of the second runner-up.

Suspense. As soon as Mr. Gooding said the name of the 1st runner-up, there were screams of excitement. The cheerleaders and members of student council rushed over to hug and congratulate me.

"Veronica Clark," Mr. Gooding boomed, "is our homecoming queen... and Antoine Mendez is the homecoming king."

Tears were streaming down my face because I just couldn't believe it. I was now a part of Fremont High School's history as the Homecoming Queen for the 1988-1989 school year. This achievement was not the result of my own efforts, but my fellow classmates' votes and belief that I should have this honor. In these many years later, I still say to all of my fellow Pathfinder alumni who voted for me -- thank you for presenting me with this memorable moment, which I continue to cherish and share with my family. Without the support of my fellow Pathfinders, I could never have done it.

Once I had reached my goal of achieving a 4.0 GPA. during my 10th grade year, I knew that I was going to be Class of 1989 valedictorian. Now and then I would wake up in the middle of the night and write down portions of my graduation speech. I did this all the way through my senior year, so that by the time they were ready to announce our class valedictorian, my speech was mostly complete.

And soon enough it was official. I had maintained the highest grade point average for my entire graduating class. By God's intervention, I had even managed to maintain a 4.0 GPA for three consecutive years. Even though I had taken Advanced Placement (AP) English and Calculus, by the grace of God I was able to excel in both of those classes because of my thirst for success. I now had the pleasure of making the graduation speech at my high school just as I had done at my junior high school. It had taken hard work, determination, diligence and faith.

But, as I stated in my valedictorian speech at my high school graduation, "If you believe it, you can achieve it." You can do this all day everyday. Make this your new motto for life.

I had never forgotten my teacher Pat back at Mid-City Alternative. But now I had a math teacher at Fremont who was another dedicated and passionate teacher. This was Mr. H. Niebergall, whom the students affectionately called "Nieb." Mr. Niebergall was such a lover of the great outdoors that on weekends he would take students hiking. He was also in charge of keeping stats for our team sports, so he would transport to the games those students who assisted him in keeping the stats. In addition, when it was time for us to prepare for the AP Calculus exam, he dedicated his lunch hour, weekday afternoons and Saturdays to tutoring those of us students who had planned on taking the exam, to ensure that we would pass.

Because I was a cheerleader, on game days I might have had to miss Mr. Niebergall's AP Calculus class since the school required that all players and cheerleaders ride the bus with the team. But Nieb arranged it so I didn't have to miss class. He would allow me to go to the games with him and the statisticians in his truck. Thanks to his dedication for math, and his love of teaching, I was able to not only master the AP exam with a passing score, but also to understand what it meant to give to others with no expectation of anything in return except the success of the one to whom you are giving. These milestones alone are gifts unto themselves.

Lesson VI: *To live is to give.*

It is because of people like Daddy, Pat and Mr. Niebergall that I learned what life is truly about. To live is to give, nothing more and nothing less. When you give to others, not only does it make you feel good, but it also makes the receiver feel good. Anyone else who witnesses the gift giving (something I learned from Dr. Wayne Dyer) will feel elated as well. As long as you are giving from your heart – "without expecting," as India.Arie says in one of her songs -- you will have a satisfaction that no monetary gift can replace. When we give to others, the act alone just opens up doors with more stuff that you can give away!

Gifts are not always in the form of material things. We all have many gifts to share, if we will only allow ourselves to realize our gifts. Many of us have the gift of listening, praying, speaking, writing, sewing, painting, and on and on. If we will only take a moment out of our hectic day to be in silence and allow God to speak to us, it is then that we will begin to realize our gifts.

One day, nearly two years after writing this portion of the book, I came upon the following passage, in what has been called one of the greatest books ever written, known to many as *The Bible*. In Romans 12 verses 6-8 it clearly states, (as taken from *The Life Connecting Bible)*:

"We all have different gifts, each of which came because of the grace God gave us. The person who has the gift of prophecy should use that gift in agreement with the faith. Anyone who has the gift of serving should serve. Anyone who has the gift of teaching should teach. Whoever has the gift of encouraging others should encourage. Whoever has the gift of giving to others should give freely. Anyone who has the gift of being a leader should try hard when he leads. Whoever has the gift of showing mercy to others should do so with joy."

Hopefully you fully understand now, if you didn't before, that as humans we are obligated to utilize our gifts in a manner that is appropriate to our lives and our life's purpose. In return we provide a benefit not only to ourselves, but also to the greater good of those within our reach. Once you realize your purpose, I implore you to harness your God-given ability, to make your positive mark upon the World.

The best lessons in life are simple and usually free. We can learn so much from each other, if we only took the time to do so. When we connect as one human to another, the experience alone is typically rewarding, and a lesson to bless our lives, if we only see it as such. As I would hear repeatedly on KCET, "It's all in how you look at it" -- whatever "it" may be.

The manner in which you think about a situation is what you will more than likely experience. My suggestion is to always think positive, and refrain from saying things that you do not wish to become true, even if it's in general conversation with someone. I know people who say, "Oh, that job is killing me." Really? Do you want the job to kill you? If not, avoid saying this expression! Another saying that is frequently heard is, "Oh, I just can't ever get ahead." Do you want to get ahead? If you do, then focus on being ahead. This logic applies for any situation in your life. "As you think, so shall you be."

During both my junior high and high school years, there was a point where I had to go and live with my Aunt Olivia, who was actually living at my Great Uncle's house. You see, Uncle Martin, who was a widower and the brother of Mama and Aunt Olivia's father, was elderly and had previously suffered a stroke. He could no longer move about on his own and was now confined to his bed. The stroke had also severely impacted the portion of the brain that controls the verbal responses, so Uncle Martin no longer had the ability to speak. When spoken to, he would respond by simply nodding his head.

During his active years, Uncle Martin had been quite a respectable man. He had migrated to California from Mississippi, worked for one of the local railroad companies in Los Angeles, and retired after many years. Having established himself in Los Angeles, Uncle Martin then invested in real estate as a way of building his assets, and secured an additional home for his son and daughter once they became adults.

I can recall the many days in which we would visit Uncle Martin and his wife, whom we affectionately called Aunt Ellen. They had nice, matching furniture, unlike our furniture at home, which mostly consisted of mismatched pieces. We children were quite proud of that, and didn't know that you could buy pieces that actually matched! In their fine living room, my siblings and I would all sit up straight on the couch. Mama had raised us to be respectful, and to mind our manners when at someone else's home. Uncle Martin and Aunt Ellen did not have a television in their living room, so we had to sit on that couch like soldiers, never daring to move, straining to exercise great self-control and discipline so we could display the most respectful and appropriate behaviors.

Visiting at our Great Aunt and Uncle's was quite a treat, however. On the coffee table in the living room, Aunt Ellen always kept a tall crystal candy dish with three separate layers. During each visit, either she or Uncle Martin would always tell us, "Go ahead, you guys can have some candy."

Upon receiving Mama's approval, we would each cautiously take just one piece -- Mama was watching our every move.

Because Uncle Martin was now disabled, it was necessary that someone remain in the house with him at all times. My Aunt Olivia discussed with Mama the possibility of having one of us stay there with her, to assist her in tending to Uncle Martin. Mama suggested to her that my oldest sister Margaret be the one. But Aunt Olivia did not like this idea. She indicated that Margaret was too much of a troublemaker. So it was that I went to stay with Aunt Olivia.

Because Aunt Olivia's house was outside of the area of my junior high school, which was now about three miles away, I had to take the street bus to and from school. Surprisingly so, this didn't bother me, nor did I allow it to disrupt my study habits. My normal homework routine continued because of my love for school and my determination to always do my best.

Prior to and subsequent to living with Aunt Olivia and Uncle Martin, there were also times when either I alone, or both my sister Peggy and I, were asked to go to Uncle Martin's house while my Aunt Olivia ran errands or had other places to go. I don't recall what I thought during those moments, but in hindsight I know that I was doing a great deed. Life is truly about giving and being of service to others. As a student during this time when I could help the family out simply by my presence in certain situations, it was a form of giving.

We never know the turn that our lives may take. Therefore, we should always be willing to lend a hand to others, especially if doing so is not going to cause us harm or to make us do without in any way. This fact takes us back to the importance of our way of thinking. If we see someone in need and only think about how we can't help him or her, this will only result in absolutely nothing occurring. But if we think of how blessed we are and realize the ways that we can support this person, if only in a small way, our endeavors will prove fruitful. For God knows all things, including the intentions in our hearts and thoughts of our minds. Think on the goodness of life, and life will be good.

Chapter 8

Fear and Turning Points

As my high-school years neared their end, it was time to decide on which college I wanted to attend. I had spent a lot of time sitting with the college counselor at Fremont, trying to decide where to apply. I cannot recall exactly how it came about, but I may have received some information from Princeton University, telling me about the school and all it had to offer. I had decided on a major of Mass Communications because of my love for speaking, reading and talking to people.

With my major in place, I decided to apply to various schools...a few of the UC's (University of California schools such as UCLA, and UC Santa Barbara), as well as the University of Southern California, Hampton University, Grambling State University and Princeton. For some strange reason I was very excited about applying to both Princeton and Hampton because I had reviewed the brochures and thought that I would really enjoy either campus. Because of the photos I saw, I was especially in awe of Princeton's campus. Whether I attended Hampton or Princeton, it would give me a new experience altogether. Not only would it provide the college experience, but also the exposure to a new state and its environment, as I had never been to New Jersey, and had spent only a brief, half-day visit to Virginia while visiting Washington D.C. with my junior high school.

Months passed and the acceptance letters started rolling in. Amazingly, I was receiving favorable responses from every college. When the envelope came from Princeton, I was filled with excitement and anticipation as I quickly ripped it open. Princeton, too, had granted me acceptance to their prestigious University. I was truly ecstatic and simultaneously in disbelief. Here I was, an African-American female from the inner city of Los Angeles who had grown up on welfare, and I had just gotten accepted to Princeton.

Immediately after reading the letter, I shared the news with my mom, only to find that she wasn't as enthused.

"I can't allow it," she told me. "You can't go to a place that I don't know nothing about. A place where we don't have any relatives close by to keep an eye on you."

I felt shattered. But after numerous discussions, Mama still remained adamant that she did not want me to attend neither Princeton nor Hampton, because we didn't have family members or friends in New Jersey or Virginia. The only out-of state-school that she agreed to allow me to attend was Grambling State University in Grambling, Louisiana. Her reasoning was because Uncle Herbert lived in New Orleans and also because Mama too had attended Grambling briefly. Uncle Herbert was my mom's youngest brother and also my favorite uncle. Although my mom meant well, she was allowing fear to keep both of us from possibly experiencing opportunities of a lifetime. But in order to maintain peace with my mother and have her blessing, I decided to attend Grambling.

The school year was now at an end and graduation day was fast approaching. Uncle Herbert flew out from New Orleans to attend and videotape my graduation.

"Are you ready for the big day?" he would ask me now and then. "Do you have your speech prepared?"

"Yes," I would always respond.

"Then recite the speech for me," he would always say. "Just to be sure."

During his annual visits with us, Uncle Herbert always demonstrated his love and affection for us by spending quality time with us. He would tell stories to my siblings and me, about when he and Mama and their siblings were kids in their small country town of Summit, Mississippi. Oftentimes he would allude to how he sometimes deliberately caused misunderstandings between his siblings and other children just to get an argument or scuffle started. He was quite a character, to say the least. Most importantly, however, the fact that he made time to come and visit us meant a lot to my siblings and me.

Graduation day for John C. Fremont High School's Class of 1989 finally arrived -- June 22. Although I was a bit nervous about my speech, I was excited to close this chapter of my life, so that a new one could begin. In addition to Uncle Herbert, other family members who gathered at the ceremony were Mama, of course, and my Aunt Olivia, who is one of Mama's two younger sisters. Aunt Olivia is the younger sister closest to Mama in age. Also in attendance was one of Mama's oldest sisters, my Aunt Janet, as well as my sisters Tanya and Peggy. We all caravanned over to the high school with great anticipation for this milestone in my life.

Before I knew it, the big moment had arrived. As I approached the podium, I could see Uncle Herbert pacing back and forth on the other side of the chain-linked fence, trying to find the perfect spot to videotape. Upon reaching the podium and acknowledging the school administration, teaching staff, parents and my fellow classmates, I launched into my speech. Here is an excerpt from the message that I left with all those who attended:

"...Yes, we must cherish our high school memories, but at the same time look ahead into our future. We cannot do so without expressing our thanks to our parents. You have guided and sacrificed for us, shed tears with us when we were sad, and laughed with us in that moment of joy. To our teachers, you have taught us to question and ask why. You have instilled in us a thirst for knowledge, and taught us that failure can be overcome. To you we say, most sincerely, Thank You.

"Our presence on this field serves as a symbol of our achievement. As we sit in our splendor and await our diplomas, I hope each of you will remember that this is not our achievement alone, but also the achievement of all those who helped us reach this point in our lives. Today, this 22nd day of June, sets us well on our way towards new beginnings. Not only are we graduating from high school, but also from childhood into adulthood. We will now make our own decisions, and do what we think is best for us. We are now at that point where we must decide between having a "good" time, and getting on that midnight train to success. We will not always have someone there to tell us what's right and what's wrong.

We must be our own leaders, and help to open doors for those young people who are to follow in our footsteps.

"We must show the people of Fremont High, South Central Los Angeles, Beverly Hills, Washington D.C., and the entire World what we're made of. Let them know that although we may argue, fuss and fight, we can also be leaders, make this World a better World, and stand up for what we know is right. I want you to prove to your fellow classmates, your parents, and most of all to yourself, that you can make a difference. But first, we must all come together as one, and be united. For no man is an island, we are our brothers' keepers. Let us live in peace and harmony, and accept each other as equals, regardless of race, color, religion or station in life. We are all going for that one major goal, and that's to be somebody, letting no man, woman, boy or girl bring us down!

"As we depart from this field today, let us not forget three important things: who we are, what we are, and who has brought us thus far. Yes, we can all go out and be somebody, but all of that glory and high honor will be overlooked if we forget where it is we came from.

"In closing, I leave each of you, my fellow classmates, with a challenge: To set your goals high, and strive hard to accomplish them. In departing, I say farewell to our Alma Mater and to our teachers and friends we leave behind. We will always remember you, because you are the ones that helped to put this knowledge into our minds. To you, the Senior Class, the achievers of tomorrow, I bid you a warm farewell and these words: 'Believe it, and you will achieve it.'

"Thank you."

Looking back on that warm summer day in 1989, I can see that there was great inspiration during our final year at Fremont, which supported my fellow senior classmates and I in reaching for our dreams. One of the mechanisms of inspiration was our school motto, which was "Find a path or make one." A second tool of inspiration was our class motto, which was "Yesterday's Dreamers, Today's Believers, Tomorrow's Achievers." These short and simple phrases provided powerful guidance that can definitely be utilized in our lives today.

When you're young, there is that tendency to take situations for granted. I can recall times when we high-school students would joke about our school motto, saying how silly we felt it to be. Now, 19 years later, I can heartily say that this small phrase finally made a great deal of sense, and can provide inspiration and guidance for all of us in our daily lives. As adults, this is what we strive to do every day: find and move along paths that were already created, or if there is no path that we wish to follow, we make our own. Either way, we keep our lives moving forward. In hindsight, as I recall these words of inspiration, I know that my senior class and I had significant words of encouragement, that would make a profound difference in our lives if only we would heed them.

With graduation over and the summer progressing, I was enjoying Southern California's warm days and getting ready for college. I had sold my Volkswagen Bug and used the funds that had been saved for me over the years to buy a Ford Bronco. I needed a more reliable vehicle that I could drive and take to Grambling. In about a month I would be on my way to Louisiana.

Then, right after my 18th birthday, another turning point in my life came.

One day while I was in my room, my mom came in with a look of distress on her face. "There's something I need to tell you," she said.

Figuring that it was nothing too drastic, I motioned for her to proceed.

My mother told me that the man whom I had called Daddy all of my life, up to this point, was not my father. My real father was not George W. Clark who died in 1983, but a man by the name of Mr. Ernest Reed who lived in Milwaukee, Wisconsin. He had a few sons who wanted to meet me. At least this was how Mama had presented it to me.

Talk about devastation! At first I didn't know what to do. But finally I did as I always had done when I was upset. I left the house. But before I did, I told my mother, "I don't care about who this man was, or the sons he has. I don't want to meet them. My daddy is dead. He's the only father I ever knew and was ever going to know!"

Jumping in my truck, I drove around with tears streaming down my face, not really knowing where to go. I cried until I didn't have any more tears left. Then I drove down to the beach (which is where I normally go now for peace and solitude when I'm feeling stressed or upset), and just sat in my car until I calmed down. Finally I drove back towards home but decided that I still wasn't ready to go there, so instead I went to visit one of my best friends, Kathryn, who lived just eight blocks from my home. I wasn't really looking for any answers. I only wanted to just share the news with someone whom I felt close to. After we talked until it was late in the evening, I finally decided to go home.

At that moment in my life, I didn't know what to think. I just kept saying to myself, "How could this be?" As time passed, my mother and I would talk briefly about it now and then.

"I didn't want to tell you," Mama confessed. "But I had to. My sisters threatened that if I didn't tell you, they would."

Eventually I learned more of the story. My biological father, Mr. Ernest Reed, Sr., had always been in contact with my aunts and would constantly ask them about my well-being. He always wanted to know if I had been told the truth. He also had a brother, Chase, who lived in Southern California and would occasionally come by to see me at my aunt's house in Compton, whenever he was called and told that I was there. Once I had graduated high school, my aunts felt that it was time for me to know.

It's amazing how life can sometimes come full circle and start to make sense to you. After I had been told about my real dad, I thought back to a day when I was about 7, after we had moved in with Daddy and had been living in his home for a while. I remember answering Daddy's telephone (because he had his own separate telephone line from us) and the voice on the other end saying, "Did your mother tell you about me?" I was puzzled and said, "No, I don't think so." My mom rushed into the room and asked me who was on the phone. I told her what the man had asked me, to which she replied, "Oh, hang up the phone -- that's probably just a wrong number." Although I never forgot that moment -- hearing my Dad's voice on the other end of the phone -- as a child I never really questioned it. All I knew was that I trusted and loved my mother. I also had Daddy in my life at the time, so to question the phone call wasn't even an afterthought.

Another incident that I recalled, once the truth had been set free, was when Daddy got sick one night and was having a heart seizure. After the paramedics had arrived at our home on 74th St., I was really paranoid and kept asking my mother, "Since Daddy has heart seizures, does this mean that I will have them too?" My mother's only response was to shun me and say, "Child, please!" As I think back on that moment I now realize that Mama was probably distraught at the fact that Daddy was very sick and she really couldn't focus on anything else... which is completely understandable.

At the same time, however, my eldest sister Margaret had heard me asking Mama this question and therefore took it upon herself to tell me, "You ain't none of Clark's child. You're Ernest's child."

I had thought to myself....huh? What? Who's Ernest? I had just brushed it off as my sister being crazy and always trying to say stuff to hurt my feelings. Now that I look back on that moment, I realize that she was only trying to give me a little bit of truth, no matter how much it may have hurt, considering that I was feeling vulnerable and weak at that moment with Daddy being sick. For as long as I can remember, I didn't like to see people have seizures, and when I did see it, I would get queasy and scared inside. I would also feel sorry for the person because the convulsions are episodes that you can't control -- it could happen to you anywhere at any given moment. This is when you have to look at your life and realize how blessed you are and pray for those around you that may be ill and need to have God's blessings upon their lives.

As time passed on, there were other incidents that I would recall, such as the times when my Dad's brother Chase would come by my aunt's house in Compton. I remember one such time when he was there and asked, "Where's my niece?" Of course, I had no clue who he was. So I would say to myself, "Hey, this guy is here to see his niece, whoever she is, so you guys better get his niece for him!" I never once considered that his niece might just be me.

Another incident happened when I was quite young, maybe about 5 or 6 (possibly even younger), when we had driven across country to Mississippi and were visiting my aunts, uncles and cousins over the summer. I remember two gentlemen coming over to my aunt's house. One of the men handed me a $10 or $20 bill. Daddy had left my aunt's house for a little while, so he didn't witness this event otherwise there might have been some altercations had he been there. I was not sure why this man was giving money to me, but figured it must have been okay since my aunts were there and didn't tell me otherwise.

So this pre-college period in the summer of 1989 was a real turning point because a part of my life that I had known to be true, was no longer the truth. So how do you move on? How do you confidently continue with life as you know it, considering that most of what you have known of it was pretty much a lie? Hey, you know what? You just do! After many moments to think about this, I eventually realized that mothers do what they feel they must do to protect their families, whether that something is right or wrong. I knew that this was the case with my mother. On the one hand my aunts were telling her that she needed to tell me who my real father was. At the same time however, my uncle Herbert, my mother's youngest brother, had warned my mother not to tell me for fear that it would cause undue harm to me and disrupt my educational triumphs.

From hindsight, I now strongly believe that Mama did what was best for everyone involved. Everything in life happens the way it is supposed to, and this was the case with my life as well.

Chapter 9

A Potential Roadblock

In a little over a month, I would leave for Grambling. Since it was a beautiful Southern California summer day, my sister Peggy, my cousin Elaine and I decided to drive to the Redondo Beach Pier in my Ford Bronco. Just before we left, Mama told me, "I don't think you should go to the beach. The truck is for going to school and not for going to unnecessary places."

"That's exactly one of the reasons we want to go," I insisted. "I'm leaving for Grambling in a few weeks. It's a really nice day, and quite honestly we don't have anything else to do except waste the day away watching television or something."

We made it safely to the beach and enjoyed spending time walking along the pier, eating and embracing the atmosphere. Then, as we were driving back, conversing about our day, my sister Peggy decided to take her son Sammuelle out of his car seat so that she could feed him, which I honestly didn't think was a good idea. We were in the far lane, traveling east on Torrance Boulevard (a 4-lane major traffic street with two lanes going east and two lanes going west), and had just crossed Madrona Avenue. Beyond the two traffic lanes, immediately to the right was a median lined with big oak trees, and then an access street for the homes that fronted to the access street.

While driving, I had nervously turned around to glance at Peggy taking Sammuelle out of the car seat. As I turned back, I noticed that traffic had apparently come to a halt. There wasn't sufficient braking room between my Bronco and the car in front of us. As I braked, I knew that we were going to rear-end the car ahead. I had always been taught that when you rear-end someone, you are automatically at fault, no questions asked. So in an attempt to avoid collision, I immediately turned the wheel of my Bronco swiftly to the right. Then…Bang!

Moments later, I awoke to the smell of ammonia being put to my nose by the paramedics. The five of us were either lying or sitting on the grass of the oak tree-lined median. Apparently, my efforts to avoid a collision had caused the Bronco to cross the lane to my right, (thankfully without hitting any cars), jump the curb and run right into one of those big oak trees on the median. After I noticed my sister Peggy holding Sammuelle in her arms, I blacked out again. During the ride to the hospital in the paramedics van, I continued to have blackout moments until Mama and Aunt Janet arrived at the hospital.

While lying on the hospital bed, slightly unconscious, I could hear my nephew wailing in the background. The nurses just couldn't seem to console him. I woke up and asked the nurses to give him to me. They were happy to do this, because they couldn't stop him from crying. Once in my arms he apparently felt better, I guess, because he was seeing a familiar face. He eventually became more calm and stopped crying.

Thankfully, none of us were seriously injured to the point of having to remain in the hospital. My injuries were probably the worst of all -- about 8 stitches on my bottom lip. I remember looking down at my shirt as a nurse was rolling me down the hospital hall, and seeing that my sleeveless sky-blue summer shirt was covered with blood. Since I have sensitivity to the sight of blood, I lost whatever it was I had eaten earlier. The nurse then had to change directions so I could get cleaned up from the new, natural design I had just added to my shirt and the rest of my outfit, which included my shorts and shoes.

The Bronco had been nearly totaled. But thank goodness, my sister Peggy, my nephew Sammuelle, my cousin Elaine and her son Kevin, were all okay. I am truly grateful that this accident didn't go any other way because I don't know how it would have affected my future had any of them (or anyone else, for that matter) gotten seriously injured as a result of my negligence.

It wasn't until Mama and I went to retrieve my truck from the Torrance Police impound garage that I realized the severity of the accident. As I approached the truck, I witnessed the front-end damage I had caused by hitting the tree. The front of the truck looked as though a giant had taken a huge baseball bat and smashed it in near the center. When I opened the driver's side door and peered inside, I noticed that the windshield was cracked in the middle. And in between the crack was a plug of my sister Peggy's hair. Upon seeing this, I thought to myself, "Oh my goodness." Since she had taken her seatbelt off, the impact of the collision must have caused her and my nephew to get thrust forward into the windshield. My heart nearly sank after viewing and realizing this. Thank God we weren't traveling any faster, because both Peggy and my nephew could have been thrown completely from the truck and into that big tree. God is good.

God is always there during the times that we need Him the most -- even though there are times when we are unable to even acknowledge the blessing because we are so consumed with the nature of whatever tragedy we are facing. In the midst of calamity, there is always some form of a godsend. We just have to calm ourselves and look at the overall picture as if we are viewing a movie. When we see events from outside of the circumstances, we will have the tendency to get an entirely different perspective.

With Providence on my side, I was able to have the stitches removed prior to my departure for school.

I now look back on this accident and wonder if I should have listened to Mama and just stayed at home. But as the saying goes, "You can't cry over spilled milk." Nor can you undo what's already been done. I have to honestly tell you that I can't regret choices that I made. The only sensible decision is to learn from the misfortune, see the lesson, whatever it may be, and embrace the enjoyable moments that I had the pleasure of experiencing prior to the setback. Catastrophes come and tribulations go, as this is a natural part of life. However, we ought to always remember to look for the hidden blessing, or sometimes the multiple blessings, that exist inside of every mountain that we must climb on our journey of life. Be not dismayed by the intense fog that may exist around the mountain, as eventually it will clear to reveal a beautiful sunlight.

Chapter 10

My College Beginnings

Despite my involvement in the accident and permanent scar that still exists today on my bottom lip, college was still my destination. My truck was unfortunately nearly totaled, so Mama and I took the Greyhound Bus to Louisiana. It took us approximately three days to get to Louisiana by bus. Since Mama had just been offered a new teaching position with Delta Sigma Theta Head Start in Los Angeles, she was unable to stay with me even for one day at Grambling while I got situated in the Martha Adams Dormitory. We took my bags up to my room, and then attended the initial orientation. Afterwards we had lunch in the cafeteria with one of my friends from Fremont, La Rhonda, and her mom. By evening Mama was on the next bus headed back to Los Angeles, so she could start her new job.

Thankfully, La Rhonda had been one of my fellow cheerleading buddies during our senior year at Fremont. Although we were only friendly acquaintances then, we definitely became good friends at

Grambling. Nevertheless, that night in my dorm room I felt all alone and scared. Here I was thousands of miles away from home with no one really to talk to. La Rhonda had relatives nearby in Shreveport, so she and her mom were staying with them for a few days while her mom was still in town. My dorm roommate was a junior and apparently wouldn't arrive until right before school began. Although there was a telephone in the room, we could only receive calls because there was no way to dial out.

Fortunately I didn't become freaked out to the point that I wanted to return home, thank goodness. I managed to fall asleep, and before I knew it, the night was over and it was a brand new day!

La Rhonda and I managed to make it successfully through enrollment, and school was now in full swing. One day while I was in my dorm room, I received a phone call from my oldest sister, Margaret.

"Are you upset at Mama because she kept the secret about your Dad all those years?" she asked me.

I thought about it for a minute. "No, I'm not upset," I said. It was occurring to me that not only does everything in life happen for a reason, but it also happens the way it is supposed to happen. " Mama had her reasons for handling this the way she did," I went on. "As her daughter I have to respect and accept that."

Being upset was not going to change the reality of the situation, so why bother harboring anger when it wouldn't do any of us involved any good? Actually, it would only make matters worse. I accepted how my mother chose to deal with it and realized that the only thing to do now was move forward with my life.

In the years to come, I got to know my Dad and his family. He was married and had three sons, all of whom were younger than me; he also had another son, from a prior relationship, who was older than me. While at Grambling that first semester, I received a telephone call from my Dad one evening while in my room, and we spoke at length for the first time. His voice sounded exactly the same as it did that day several years ago when he had called our home and I had answered the telephone.

"I'd like you to spend Thanksgiving with me and my family," he said, "so you can get a chance to meet all of them. I'm going to send you a round-trip plane ticket."

It was during that Thanksgiving visit that I got to know my brothers and my Dad's wife Linda, who (unbeknownst to me at the time) was white. (This didn't matter to me however, because in reality I was in awe at the diversity of my newfound family). Wow! I now had a whole new family in addition to the one back in California. How blessed is that!

During this visit I became well acquainted with all of my brothers. It was also during this particular visit that one night, while my Dad and I were up late, (as we did just about every night that I was there, trying to do some catching up), he asked me, "Did you ever wonder about where or who your dad was? Why didn't you ever ask your mother about me?"

This question came as quite a shock to me, and created some discomfort. You see, I didn't know how to tell him that the reason I never wondered about my "father" or "dad" was because I did have a father who was there for me during my younger years, and was a tremendous part of my life, even long after he had died. Although this was the truth, I didn't want to hurt his feelings. So I just told him, "No, I didn't wonder or question Mama about my father."

During another one of those late-night talks, my Dad told me that his family, my brothers included, always knew about me and that I should never feel that I wasn't loved because I was. "I told your brothers as soon as they were old enough to understand, that they had a sister," he said.

I never really understood why he shared this with me because it didn't really matter. It was all in the past. What mattered most was that we were now all united and would hopefully have a growing relationship together from this point forward.

From that period in November 1989, I went on to build a relationship with my Dad and his family. Just about every Sunday, I would receive a telephone call from Dad. When time permitted, I would also go and visit them during my college summer breaks. It was wonderful to get closer with one of my brothers, Melvin, who was the oldest of the three sons from my dad's marriage. Melvin and I would spend lots of time together, since he had his driver's license, which permitted us to go to different places around the city. This time together allowed the two of us to be ourselves and say whatever was on our minds.

I remember asking Melvin, "How would you have reacted to me if I had been a different type of person -- a little more rough around the edges?" In other words, I wanted to know how he would have felt if I had been more like a "hood rat" rather than someone with manners who also loved school.

He politely answered, "In that case, I probably wouldn't spend any extra time with you, other than general family time with the rest of the family. I definitely wouldn't take you anywhere."

"Hey, I can understand that!" I told him.

As I spent more time with Dad and the family, he always made it a point to reassure me that his family always knew about me so I shouldn't ever feel that I wasn't wanted. As time passed, this was hard for me to digest because other sources in the family had told me that my brothers didn't find out about me until I was on *Wheel of*

Fortune. Knowing this always created a question in my mind about the validity of Dad's declarations that my brothers always knew they had a sister. Since I am not the confrontational type, I never asked Dad to clarify what he meant. On top of not wanting to stir up conflicts within the family, I also never wanted to ask because in reality, what difference did it make anyway? Again, the main point was, we now had positive relationships with one another so this was really and truly all that mattered. As the title of the famous book goes, "Don't Sweat the Small Stuff!" Because doing so only creates unnecessary headache and unwarranted stress.

Considering that I was always getting different stories about my mother and father's relationship during the time that I was conceived, I eventually realized that there was the strong possibility that I was a mistake -- an accident that shouldn't have happened. But it also occurred to me that, in this life of ours that is orchestrated by God, there are no "mistakes" and no "accidents." There may be human mistakes, but through God's eyes, mistakes are nonexistent. I know that although I was probably the mistake of Mama and Dad who are purely human, it was God's intention that I be created. I strongly believe that a large part of God's intent (which is called my purpose) for my being created was so that I could help others in different aspects of their lives.

So if someone has ever told you that you were a mistake or an accident, be reassured that this is true only in his or her small human world. In God's infinite World you were put here on this Earth for not one reason, but several. Hopefully you will embark upon a quest to determine what those reasons are, because leaving your bona-fide purpose unfulfilled truly makes your life incomplete. I also encourage you to always remain curious about your life. It is the quest for continued knowledge about yourself that molds you to be the person you were destined to become.

Now that all of my brothers and I are grown and living our own lives, we still get together for Thanksgiving whenever we can. Although it was almost 18 years ago when I first met my Dad and his family, I am still learning how to find my place within the Reed family. This is something that only time will mend and bring together. If you find yourself in a similar situation, what I have found is that the more you feel good about who you are, despite your circumstances, the better life will become for you, regardless of the events that have brought you to this point. The key is focusing on that which is positive and learning from the negative experiences. Focusing on the positive is like holding fast to your dreams.

Stay in a "can do" frame of mind and nothing will be impossible as long as you know that you have a Universal God who is everywhere, ready, willing and able to fight any battles or obstacles that you might meet along the way.

Chapter 11

College and More Turning Points

Lesson VII: *Optimism and Intrinsic Motivation are Keys to Success*

Although I enjoyed my studies and personal growth at Grambling, I also needed a job to keep some change in my pocket. The only type of work you could do in Grambling, Louisiana was at the school since it was pretty much all there was to the City of Grambling. If you worked at the school, it was considered work-study which would go towards your education. My education was completely paid for, including books, because of various scholarships and grants that I was able to get. However, since I was living away from home, I still needed bare necessities to keep it all together. I knew that my mom didn't have money to send to me, so the only other alternative was to get a job.

When I went home to L.A. for Christmas break and saw how La Keesha was able to work and go to school and have a nice car to drive,

I figured I had better do the same thing. So I returned to Grambling, collected all of my belongings and came home again. My plan was to transfer to Cal State University Dominguez Hills (CSUDH), which was one of the other universities where I had previously been accepted. That way, I could re-apply for a job at Bank of America. In January of 1990, this is exactly what I did, and continued to work and go to school throughout my entire academic career at CSUDH.

Along the way, I changed my major from Mass Communications to Psychology because of my growing interest in what goes on in the minds of children.

But my progress wasn't as smooth as I would have liked for it to be. In my junior year at CSUDH, Mama had some financial troubles, and as a result she lost the duplex property we were living in on 56th St in Los Angeles. (This was also the prior home of my great Uncle Martin and his wife Aunt Ellen. Mama had purchased the home after Uncle Martin passed away.) She had refinanced the mortgage with a guy whom I didn't trust. However, despite my repeated objections to the refinance deal, Mama did it anyways. As a result, Mama could no longer afford the payments and lost the property to foreclosure. We had no place else to go except our old home on 74th St. (Daddy's house), which Mama still owned but had rented out.

Since Mama had rented the property to someone who had lost themselves to drugs, the house suffered some neglect. The carpet needed replacing badly, and it was going to take some time for Mama to get the money to do the necessary repairs to make the house livable again, at least to our standards. I told Mama that I couldn't live there till it was fixed up.

While the house was being repaired, Mama lived with my sister Tanya and her family. I spent the night with different friends, including my boyfriend at the time, while he rented an apartment with a friend of his. I didn't enjoy being a wanderer with no place to call home. So finally I had the guts to ask La Keesha's parents if I could live with them until I found an apartment to rent. Thankfully they agreed, and this is what I did for about one month, until I found my first apartment. But things weren't smooth sailing at La Keesha's either. Early one night, I returned to La Keesha's house only to find that no one would answer the door, despite the fact that everyone's car was in the driveway.

I rang the doorbell several times and even knocked a few times, but there was no answer. I didn't know what to do. Then, remembering that there was a Hampton Inn about 2 miles north of there, I jumped into my 1990 Ford Escort and headed to the hotel.

After checking in and finding my way to the room, I just sat on the bed wondering why no one had answered the door, even though it was obvious that they were at home. I'm not sure whether they felt I had come home too late, although it was somewhere between 8:30 and 9:30 p.m. The reasons no one answered were definitely unclear. However, that was the least of my worries at this point. My period had started, which was always irregular, so I just never knew when it was going to show up. Now here I was in a hotel room with no protection and no change of underwear. I utilized the hotel towels temporarily until I could get to a store and purchase the necessary female hygiene products.

That night became a vivid memory. I felt alone, just as I did that first night in my dormitory at Grambling, after Mama had left. However, I just went into a survivor type mode and did what needed to be done until a new day arose.

The following day, when I went back to La Keesha's house, I told them that I had been knocking and ringing the doorbell the previous night. They all said that they were there but just didn't hear the doorbell or the knocks. Regardless of whether they did or not, I knew that I had to find an apartment pronto, and I did! It was a bachelor-style apartment with a bedroom, small kitchenette, and ¾ bathroom (a sink, toilet and shower only—no tub), in the city of Hawthorne.

I was very excited to finally have a place to call my own. Although the circumstances that brought me to this point were difficult, I was enjoying the fact that I was now officially on my own, which is the best feeling that a single female can have. At the time I had just one goal in mind, and that was to obtain my bachelor's degree and move on to the next phase of my life.

At this point I was now working as a clerical specialist in the Appraisal Department for Bank of America. This was a switch from the initial job that I had when I first returned to Bank of America. You see, when I came back from Grambling and began working for Bank of America once again, I worked for the Proofing Department on weeknights from about 4 p.m. until 10 p.m. After I had worked in this department for about 2 and a half years, the classes that I now needed for school were mainly being offered in the evening. It was therefore necessary that I look for a day position at the bank, which is how I came to work in the Appraisal Department. While I was working as a clerical specialist in the Appraisal Department in Gardena, a point came when a class that I needed to take was only offered during the day while I was at work. I discussed this with my manager, Ken, who was the district manager of the Appraisal Department. He gave me permission to take an extended lunch on the days that I had class, and attend the class during my lunch break.

Wow! Talk about an awesome manager! How many managers today would allow something like that? If you are a manager and you're saying to yourself, "I'd allow that, especially if the employee is a good worker," you are one darn good manager. May you continue to think outside of the box, and help people along the way!

This is just the type of manager that Ken was. He always wanted to help others succeed, and therefore if I needed to take that class at that time, then by all means, was his attitude. To this very day, I am grateful to Ken, the best manager I have ever worked for, who became a "father figure at work" for me. When Mama lost the house and we had to quickly gather our belongings, Ken allowed me to leave work early so that I could get all of my things before the property was locked and we would no longer have access to the house. Later, when my husband and I were having problems, Ken was always there to encourage me to hang in there, because the best was yet to come. Ken remained my manager for over ten years. To this very day, he and his family still remain an extended part of my family.

The day finally came when I had completed all the requirements to graduate from CSUDH. I had managed to maintain a grade point average of 3.3 (I was .10 points away from making the Dean's List!), despite the challenges that met me along the way. My experiences had only taught me that challenges truly make you stronger, and hopefully more determined. When you have a goal, let nothing stop you at accomplishing it, because the feeling of achievement is one that cannot be bought, especially when you've truly earned it.

In late Spring of 1993, I received my Bachelor of Arts Degree in Psychology.

Chapter 12

Life Beyond College

At this point I was still living in my apartment, and had broken up with my boyfriend Daniel earlier in the year. I was therefore quite surprised to see his youngest sister Rashida at the graduation. She came over and told me, "Daniel's here with me. He wants to see you. Is it okay for him to come over and speak with you?"

Daniel had always held a special place in my heart; however, because of the circumstances of the breakup, my stubbornness and mixed-up emotions, I wasn't sure how I'd feel about seeing him, knowing that we weren't together. Daniel had to know how much I truly loved him, but at that moment, my heart was still in pain.

"No, I don't want to see him," I told Rashida.

My Dad was standing next to me. When Rashida left, he said to me, "Your mind is saying no, but your heart is saying something else."

And boy, was he right. God knows that I really wanted to see Daniel and give him a big hug and kiss, but I just couldn't bring myself to allow it at that moment.

A few months later, my wounds began to heal, and Daniel resurfaced again, only this time it was at my front door. He told me, "Look...we should be together; and eventually I want to marry you."

After several walks and talks, we agreed that we both truly wanted to be together. Shortly after, he moved into my small apartment, only because we had planned on getting married later. And this is exactly what we did.

Now that I had graduated, I was still working in the Appraisal Department at Bank of America. With my degree in Psychology, I had made a number of attempts to land jobs working with children in that field, but had not been hired. Ken told me that he thought it would be a good idea if I became a Bank of America appraiser. He felt that I would do very well as such and wanted to recommend me for the bank's Appraisal Training program. Before getting into the program however, I had to go to appraisal school to get my Provisional License. With Daniel's encouragement and financial assistance, in August of 1993, I enrolled in a 3-month licensing program at Miller Real Estate School in nearby Granada Hills, where classes were held only on the weekends. I successfully completed all of the required courses and later went on to pass the State exam.

Lesson VIII: *God always places people around us to help guide us.*

One of the senior appraisers at my office, Wendy, offered to allow me to go out with her on the weekend, to a few inspections -- just to see how I would like it. This would be voluntary for both of us.

Wendy would receive no additional pay for providing me with pre-training, and I wouldn't get paid for going out on these inspections either. Each Saturday for about three or four weeks, we met at various properties. I knew that this was a great opportunity to get firsthand training in the appraisal profession from one of the best appraisers at our office, and I was not going to decline this blessing. After doing that for a few weeks, Wendy informed Ken that I should apply for the training program and that she would recommend me.

Ironically, just at that moment, it appeared that I might finally be hired as a counselor visiting children's group homes. Almost simultaneously, I got accepted into the Appraisal Training Program at Bank of America, and that was the road I chose. For the next 10 years, I would never look back.

When I returned from the Training Program, Wendy was assigned as my Mentor-Appraiser and trainer.

Wendy would now be added to my list of people that made a positive impact on my life. Not only did she teach me to become a successful appraiser, she also taught me the importance of investing in my 401k and buying real estate. Wendy always took time out to show me various investments and the benefit of owning rental properties such as 2-4 units. I was able to amass a sizeable retirement plan over a 10-year period.

I would therefore encourage you to invest fully in your 401k plan at work, if you're fortunate to have one at your company. If your company matches the contributions that you make, up to a certain point, see to it that you contribute at least the amount that they will match. For instance, if your company will match your contributions up to 4%, then at a minimum, make sure that you are contributing at least 4% of your income. By not doing so, you are cheating yourself out of free money. Look at it this way; your company will only invest extra money in you, if you're willing to first invest in yourself!

Like Ken, Mr. Niebergall and Pat, Wendy helped me to become who and what I am today. Again, it is about listening to those closest to you who have a genuine interest in your success. Take the advice and utilize it. Not only will it make a huge, positive difference in your life, but it will also allow the person helping you, to feel good about their deeds.

In the spring of 1994, Daniel and I got officially engaged, with a wedding date in early September. About the same time, I successfully completed the Appraisal Training at Bank of America and officially became an appraiser.

Not long after Daniel and I got engaged and shared the news of our engagement with my family, some strange events began to take place. One day Daniel and I went to visit my mother at her home in Los Angeles. Upon arriving, we were shocked to find that dry cereal had been spilled all over the interior of the house, mostly on the living-room and dining-room floor and parts of the front bedroom. (In order to protect the privacy of this family member the name has been subsequently changed). When I asked my mother what happened, she said that one of my relatives, whom we will just call "Lacy" "…went into a rage after we had a disagreement. She took the cereal and threw it around the house like a mad woman." My mother appeared quite distressed and was trying to put the house back in order. Daniel and I helped her clean up in an attempt to restore peace and calmness.

This event would be the start of even more chaos in the near future. Initially when Lacy had gotten married, she moved out of the Los Angeles area with her husband, but recently she had become estranged from him, and moved in with Mama. Now Lacy was seeking to destroy my mother's good name amongst anyone and everyone who knew her. She had decided to tell all the people in my mother's world that Daddy (Clark) had molested her. She went through Mama's phone book and called Mama's closest friends and our relatives with this horrible allegation.

My mind swirled with questions. Never had there been any indication that something like this was happening between Daddy and Lacy. Why would a victim of sexual abuse choose to broadcast something that was so blatantly hurtful not only to herself but to everyone she and the family knows? From my studies in psychology and sociology, I learned that most victims of abuse would hide the facts of their torment for as long as they possibly can. Victims of sexual abuse oftentimes feel ashamed or embarrassed, and usually have a fear of others finding out about their experience. Well, this was far from what Lacy was doing. So I suspected that there was not much truth in her allegations.

From this scenario, Lacy went on to accuse our brother Charles of physically assaulting her, and therefore requested a restraining order against him. Since she was living with Mama at the time, the restraining order – if it was granted -- would mean that Charles could no longer come to Mama's house as long as Lacy was there. Fortunately the judge dismissed Lacy's request, finding that it was unwarranted, mainly because a few days after filing for a restraining order against Charles, she requested a second restraining order against Mama. The judge told Lacy that he would not grant the request because she was living in Mama's house. If she wanted Mama to stay away from her, then she (Lacy) would need to move out of Mama's house.

We were all very grateful for the judge's ruling on the matter. About this time, there were other incidents involving Lacy, my sister Tanya, and Tanya's husband. There were no restraining orders granted, but quite a bit of chaos occurred -- which gave me reason to keep my distance from the family for a while until some resemblance of peace returned. Eventually Lacy reconciled with her husband and moved out of Mama's house.

Despite all this turmoil, Daniel and I got married as planned in September. Six months later, we found out that we would be having our first child. A year and a half after we were married, God blessed us with a beautiful daughter, Little Miss Neemah. From that moment forward we became a family of three.

Chapter 13

More College, and Then AIDS

Lesson IX: *God gives us all freedom of choice and free will.*

I'm not special, nor am I different than anyone else on Earth, except for the fact that I, by some miracle, have listened to God's direction in my life. Sometimes I didn't want to accept certain responsibilities because doing so would interrupt my lifestyle and plans for my life. But instead of resisting God's messages, I would give in—not knowing at the time that it was His direction I was following. Here's another example:

In 1996 my sister Peggy called a meeting for our entire immediate family.

For some weird reason, I already had a feeling as to why Peggy was calling this meeting but I didn't want to believe it when the thought entered my mind. As it turned out, I was right. Peggy had been given the heartbreaking, life-changing news that she was HIV positive and she needed to let the family know.

"And in the event of my death," she said, "my husband and I want you, Veronica, and Daniel to take the kids."

Well, that was hard to swallow since my husband and I had just recently become parents. At the time our daughter was only about 4 months old, while my niece and nephew were 3 and 6 years of age, respectively. We had also only been married just over a year and a half, so why did she want us to take the kids, especially considering the reality that I was the youngest in our family? There were two other sisters in the family, both of whom were older than me and also married, so why couldn't they take them? Not only do we have two sisters but we also had a mother who was still alive and well, healthy and strong -- a mother who actually suggested to Peggy during the meeting that she let her take the kids if something should happen to her.

But Peggy refused. "The kids need a caregiver who is young," she said. "Mama is too old to care for the kids."

At the time, all I wanted to focus on was my sister's HIV status and her need of support from her family. I didn't want to focus on a debate about who was going to care for her children. So, of course, after many long discussions and disagreements with my husband, we agreed to my sister's request. In the event that Peggy died, we would be the legal guardians of my niece and nephew.

How had I already known what Peggy was going to tell us? It is because in life, you have to listen when you're being spoken to. There are also occasions when you must listen to what your family is telling you, particularly when the information is for your well-being.

My mother had received two disturbing phone calls from a young lady who told her that Peggy's husband had given her a disease. It is unknown whether or not he had given it to her before my sister's marriage or after, but she called my mother on several occasions in hopes that my mother would relay the message to Peggy.

My mother and my sister Tanya told Peggy about the young lady and the misfortune that her husband had left her with, but Peggy wouldn't believe it. She continued to deny it even after she was given her diagnosis in 1996. Because she was an abused wife, she continued to believe what her husband repeatedly told her, that *she* had given the disease to him! If only Peggy had listened when Tanya and my mother continuously told her that her husband had given some young lady a horrible disease, we all might have been spared the tragedy that the future held. Sometime between 1998 and 1999, Peggy developed full blown Acquired Immune Deficiency Syndrome, better known as AIDS.

Even after a few years of knowing that her husband had knowingly given her HIV, Peggy continued to defend him and would become angry with our family because we didn't want him around. How is it that someone only focuses on their "supposed" love for a person when that person truly does not love them back? Yet all the while this person whom they love is abusing and disrespecting not only them but their children as well. How does this happen?

Low self-esteem is part of the reason that this happens. When a woman thinks very little of herself, she will allow others to take advantage of her because she feels that this is the only way to get them to like her. This is very far from the truth. In reality, the less you think of yourself, the less that others will think of you as well. If you think highly of yourself (not necessarily in arrogance), others will think highly of you also. This is called the power of attraction. The people whom you attract into your life will feel the same way about you as you feel about yourself. However *you* think and feel about yourself, these will be the types of people that you will attract into your life. Feel good about who you are, and the people that come into your life will feel good about you too.

Right now, no matter how far you feel you are from being where you would like to be, the steps to get there can be taken at this very moment. Say to yourself, "I like myself. I like myself. I am strong. I am strong. I am talented. I am talented," and continue to repeat this every morning when you wake up and each night before you go to bed. By doing this you will bring these characteristics into existence and with God's guidance you are capable of controlling your own life.

After repeating these statements, pray the following prayer (taken in part from The Prayer of Jabez): "Heavenly Father, strengthen me to be who you want me to be. Bless me indeed so that I may be a blessing to someone else. Enlarge my territory. That Your hand will be with me and that You would keep me from evil, that I might not cause pain, but I will be used as an instrument of thy peace." If you know what it is you would like to be, then replace "who you want me to be" with what you want to be in that space. For instance, if you want to be a good mother, make the statement "Heavenly Father, strengthen me to be a good mother." Also, add the following statement to your morning and nightly routine, "I am a good mother." Know without a doubt that this shall come to pass.

I assure you that if you continue to make these affirmations and pray this prayer, you will see great, positive change in your life.

Chapter 14

A Blessing and a Curse

How is it that two sisters who came from the same mother's womb, who grew up in the same home and were raised by the same mother, could be so different?

There are a few reasons for this. Peggy's diminishing self-esteem first began because of the touch of a man -- the man whom I called Daddy for most of my young life. Daddy was sunshine on my rainy days, and thunder on Peggy's.

My dad was part of the reason that for the first few years of my life I strove only for excellence in school. Each time that I brought home a report card with all A's, he would take me to McDonalds as a treat. In all of my elementary years, A's got me rewarded with a McDonald's cheeseburger, small fries, and my favorite of the whole meal....a vanilla shake!

My dad was also a strong influence on my monetary beliefs. He always told me to "be independent." He would tell me to make sure that I could provide my own way in life, especially financially. He would tell me to always have my own money so that I would not have to rely on others for anything. He often told me "You only need one credit card. Use it for emergency purposes only. Pay cash for everything so that you don't ever have any unnecessary bills." I was quite young when Daddy told me this, maybe about 7 or 8. But the advice stuck!

Because I listened to Daddy, I was able to maintain good credit and buy everything for myself starting from the time that I had my first job and earned my first paycheck at age 15. Daddy's advice has stuck with me to this very day.

But Peggy, as well as my other sister Tanya, didn't get these special lessons on life, at least as far as I know they didn't -- in fact, they were dealt just the opposite.

You see, the man whom I called Daddy was also an alcoholic. But that wasn't his main weakness. He would also physically touch my sisters in ways which no man should ever touch children under 18, nor touch *any* person who isn't in agreement with the sexual acts, regardless of their age. So, while Daddy was *my* hero, he was my sisters' worst nightmare. By touching them inappropriately, he caused great damage to their lives, and also to mine in some ways.

I can remember a day when I was about five or six. I walked into the kitchen of our rented home on 69th Street and saw Daddy standing behind one of my sisters. His hands were underneath her shirt, fondling her breasts. It's very interesting when I look back on that moment. This is a memory that I can see quite vividly in my mind right now, as clear as the words on this page. At age 5, I didn't know a whole lot, but there was something about what I saw that wasn't right, though I wasn't sure what it was. Nor would I ever tell my mother because I was only 5, so I didn't know that what I saw was wrong and extremely detrimental, and needed to be stopped.

I can remember another night when my mother was away from home, possibly at choir rehearsal, which is where she went just about every Thursday night. I heard my sister Peggy saying aloud, "...Stop...stop!" At the time I didn't know why she was saying that because I was in the bedroom that she and I shared, and she was in the kitchen. Not till I was older, and Daddy was dead and gone, did I realize he had possibly molested all of my sisters. The interesting thing is this: never ever, in all the times that I was alone with him, did he ever touch me inappropriately.

Unfortunately I can't say the same for my sisters, but the impact on their lives was quite devastating. Because of the molesting that they had endured, they would go on to relationships with abusive men, adding to their already inhibited self-esteem and self-image. You could say that Daddy may have damaged a few lives, and enhanced one: mine. He was both a blessing and a curse. But it is my firm belief that my life was spared because of God's divine intervention and protection.

Why He didn't protect my sisters is somewhat unknown to me, but something I will definitely ask should I ever get the opportunity. However, I can think of a few reasons why I was protected and left "untouched."

The first reason could have possibly been because, as a child (since I had been raised in a Christian church from birth), I always felt that God was with me. Every night when we were growing up, our mother would make us say our prayers together as a family. She would lead the prayer, and my siblings and I would repeat the words that she would say. We did this every night that I can remember, I believe, until I was in junior high school. By this time the tradition was written in stone upon my heart, so I continued on my own to pray every night before I went to bed. And I continue to do this today, asking God to watch over and protect my family and me. In my heart, I truly believe that this was probably one of the reasons I was spared. It was my unspoken faith in God that shielded me from harm.

The second reason: I strongly believe that God knew that someone (at least one of my mother's children) had to be given the ability to care for our mother, as she got older. I'm guessing that God saw fit for me to take on a portion of this role. Why God chose me is unknown to me. However, I do know that I have assumed that role to a strong degree, and listened to God's instructions. Perhaps God knew that I would do as He commanded me to do, even though it was not always easy. But I heeded a saying that I have often repeated to myself over the years, "Anything worth having is worth working for." I love my mother and with God's blessings, will do whatever it takes to make sure that she is happy and healthy.

There were many days when I was alone with Daddy, but he never even attempted to touch me inappropriately. At the time, Daddy lived alone in his house on 74th street in Los Angeles. On many of the Fridays that he would take me to McDonald's, we would go back to his house afterwards. While there, I would go outside and catch butterflies that would gracefully land on a flowery bush in front of the house. One day while I was doing this, a little girl who lived across the street came over to catch butterflies with me. After that, every time that I went to Daddy's house, I would catch butterflies with the neighbor across the street. Whenever I was inside Daddy's house, I would either watch television (which wasn't too often) or read any book that I could find, which was frequently a copy of *The Reader's Digest*.

On many days, Daddy would also pick me up from school. Our normal routine would be to stop by the liquor store on the way home so that he could get his whisky (I.W. Harper) or Schlitz beer. He would always tell me to get whatever I wanted and that would normally be a banana Suzi Q and a can of Hi C punch. Talk about sugar overload! That's a combination of items that I wouldn't dare allow my daughter to eat now!

Lesson X: *Everything happens for a reason.*

Witnessing some of the molestation and coming to the realization that my sisters had been molested, was deeply traumatic. It could have haunted me for the rest of my life, or it could have made me stronger and wiser.

What I learned, eventually, was that in order to successfully overcome the pain and trauma that all of us girls suffered, it was important for me to go within myself and forgive the person who caused us such great harm. Of course, Daddy was dead, so I couldn't talk to him face to face. But I realized that there was power in visualizing myself talking to Daddy, letting him know how I felt -- letting him know how his inappropriate actions had affected my life. And in the end, as I close my experience, tell Daddy that I forgive him.

This was eventually my mindset towards Peggy's ex-husband. I knew that holding on to my anger against him wouldn't solve anything, nor could it change the events of her life. It occurred to me that in order to move on successfully, I had to forgive him and just hope and pray that he didn't cause anyone else and their family, the type of pain and suffering we as a family have endured. Forgiveness is crucial to healing.

I've always believed that *everything* that happens in your life happens for a reason. In every situation whether good or bad, there is a lesson to be learned. In a good situation it's not much of a challenge to see the lesson. Nor are you even looking for any lesson because you're just enjoying the moment, which is exactly what you should do. But also in every good situation, the lesson to learn is to not only enjoy it, but to appreciate that moment.

You would be surprised at how many people in the world don't know how to appreciate a good moment or situation. Sometimes people are so filled with unhappiness that, no matter how good their lives are at any given moment, they will find something to feel bad about. They will search to find that one thing that can get them upset or cause them to feel down.

In fact, I have found that some people feel as though they *must* have something to complain about, whether it's warranted or not. So enjoy the goodness that life presents to you. Trials and challenges will come soon enough. Be sure to stay in the moment and enjoy life when it offers you the present of laughter and good times, because heartache could be right around the corner.

Chapter 15

Learning How to Forgive

When I finally realized that Daddy --my Hero -- had molested my sisters and my mind was getting the best of me, I prayed for forgiveness for Daddy because I knew that he had to be sorry for what he had done. I didn't think he was sorry just because I felt he should be, but I knew he was sorry because he was a man who had a heart of gold. He would give to anyone and everyone around him.

However, molesting my sisters was his human weakness and downfall, and something my mother and I deeply believe he eventually paid for when his leg was amputated as a result of his foot developing an infection. I know some of you may think that this is not punishment enough, but if you knew Daddy and his passion for driving a truck, then you would know that this was almost like a death sentence. A few years after having his leg amputated, Daddy died.

Despite the fact that Daddy molested my sisters -- and I can't tell you often enough how sorry I am that he did this -- I still choose to remember him as the kind and loving spirit who would give you the shirt off of his back. I know many of you are thinking, "Yeah that is easy for you to say because you weren't the one being molested." But I ask you, what good would it do if I only held remorse and distaste for Daddy? What good would it do if every time I thought about him, it were the image of him engaged with my sister during my childhood years? I ask you, what good does that do? To think only about the negative aspects of my time with him would be absurd. Not to mention that it would only cause me more trauma and disgust. Why put myself through that, when I still have to deal with life in the present moment?

Lesson XI: *Focus on that which is positive.*

Instead, I choose to remember the happy and joyous times we had, like the summer trips when he and Mama would drive us across country from Los Angeles to Mississippi to visit our relatives. The times when he would go to the liquor store and buy treats for not just all five of us siblings, but half the children who lived on our street. You see Daddy was my first example of what it meant to be giving and expect nothing in return. When we lived at our old house on 69th St., all the kids on the block were happy when he came around because they knew that he would provide treats for everyone.

I also like remembering how he gave us siblings our first driving lessons in his car. I must have been between five and eight years old when he gave me the first lesson! I like remembering his smile and all of these special moments.

And no, I'm not saying that these happy moments are more important than the trauma he put my sisters through. But I am saying that this is how I choose to remember Daddy, because it leaves me with many feelings of happiness and joy. Life is too short to spend it being disgusted and remorseful. And remembering only the unhappy moments can also be a very tiring and unpleasant experience. I don't know about you, but in my eyes life is too beautiful to be unpleasant!

I share this with you because we all experience crap in our lives. But it's how you deal with the crap that will either make you or break you.

If you've had negative experiences in your life, I ask you to learn from them and may they only be lessons for your life and not your life-lesson. If you allow them the power to act only as lessons, then that is all the power they will have. But on the other hand, if you allow them to be your Life-Lesson, then you've given them power to take over your life. I've chosen many times, and still continue to choose, the former because the latter can only take me so far and create misery in my life. By using negative experiences as lessons, I am able to move on in life with a positive outlook, knowing that I have truly learned from this and am happy to know that it won't happen to me twice!

Look at it this way: if those events had never occurred, I probably wouldn't be sharing these thoughts of hope with you right now.

So from this moment forward, make a vow to yourself to focus on the lesson in every negative situation and allow it to be only that: A Lesson! Treasure the positive moments, and utilize them to get you through the tough times.

Chapter 16

Graduate School

After I had begun my career as a residential real-estate appraiser with Bank of America during the spring of 1994, I encouraged Daniel to go back and finish his undergraduate education and obtain his Bachelor's Degree.

Daniel had previously attended California State University at Long Beach (CSULB), although his dream had been to attend Morehouse College in Atlanta, Georgia. Unfortunately he had dropped out of CSULB after his second year, due to financial hardships and family commitments, which came as a result of him helping his mom to care for his two younger sisters (as he had done since the age of 7). Daniel eventually had to move in with his grandparents, and continued to work part-time as a Special Education assistant for the Los Angeles Unified School District (LAUSD) while he attempted to pay off some of his debt. Daniel was fortunate to have a good friend whose mom worked for the LAUSD. She was able to get him a job at her school. This is where his career with the school district began, and he remained there until after he received his Bachelor's degree.

Daniel and I had agreed that after he received his B.A., I would be able to go back to school to get my Masters Degree. In the Spring of 1997, Daniel graduated from CSUDH after many challenges that come with being a working husband and a new dad. His B.A. was in Liberal Studies, since it was his goal to become a teacher, as he was currently working as a teacher's assistant. Upon graduating, Daniel secured his first position as a teacher with the school district.

A year later, Daniel and I were able to buy our first home not too far from my office; we would live there for the next 5 years. About this time, the local real estate market surged with activity, marking the beginning of a 9-year appreciation period. Needless to say, business picked up at Bank of America, and I found myself starting to work 10-12 hours per day. In all honesty, during the first 3 years, it didn't feel like I worked that amount of hours since I completely enjoyed what I was doing.

Two years had gone by since Daniel had received his Bachelors, so we decided that it was now time that I pursued my graduate education, especially since I really didn't want to continue working over 60 hours per week with minimal time to spend with Daniel and Neemah. In the fall of 1999, I applied to the Fully Employed Masters of Business Administration (FEMBA) program at Pepperdine University's Graziadio School of Business and Management. In March of 2000, Pepperdine wrote to me saying that I had been accepted.

That summer, my Pepperdine journey began.

In my first trimester, I enrolled in the mandatory course for beginning students, namely Human Behavior of Organizations, along with Statistics/Research Methods. I was so excited to be in graduate school that it never crossed my mind that I was taking on two courses. It had been seven years since my previous college study; in those days, though I was still working full time, I was responsible only for myself. Now I was embarking on an even greater collegiate challenge. Not only was I working approximately 10-12 hours per day, but I was also a wife and mother of a 5-year old daughter. As if that wasn't plenty, my husband and I also had joint custody (with my sister Peggy) of her two children, my niece and nephew. Because my sister's health was still fairly decent, it never occurred to me that there might come a time when she too might need me.

One day while I was working from home, the doorbell rang. It was my sister Peggy. She was now working as a school bus driver, and her bus route was nearby. She had stopped by because she wasn't feeling too good and needed to lie down for a while. After Peggy had taken a nap for about 30-45 minutes she felt slightly rested. Shortly thereafter, she invaded my refrigerator and then headed back out to work.

When Peggy invaded our refrigerator, she was looking for any leftover banana pudding -- I was known to make this quite well -- or mustard greens. Peggy wasn't much of a vegetable eater, but she loved my mustard greens! I would make them for her under one condition: she had to buy the fresh greens and then I would make them for her sometime during the next week. I actually didn't mind making the greens because the satisfaction that I got from watching her enjoying them was priceless, as anyone who enjoys cooking can probably attest to.

This time, however, Peggy's surprise visit was to be my first indicator that her immune system was beginning to falter. As the year progressed, her health became more unpredictable, with periods of hospitalization at St. Francis Medical Center in Lynwood whenever she had neglected to take her medication. During the infrequent periods that her husband would leave her for days and weeks at a time, Peggy would go on these non-medication binges.

Each time she was hospitalized, my mother and I would go see her on alternate days. This was a bit of a challenge for me considering my heavy workload, responsibilities at home and graduate school. Thankfully I only had class one night per week, with group meetings on the weekends. Although there were many days when I truly didn't feel up to it, I couldn't let Mama and Peggy down. I would schedule time, either between my appraisal appointments or immediately afterwards, to go by the hospital.

At one point when Peggy was hospitalized, we had to have my nephew Sammuelle (Peggy's son) stay with us since the school that he was attending, was down the street from our house. Although Peggy and her family lived 10-12 miles north of our house, Sammuelle was attending the middle school in our community because of his unfortunate luck at the local middle school he was attending in his own neighborhood. Frequently, during his walks to school, some kids would bully him by taking his lunch money and harassing him. As a result, Peggy enrolled Sammuelle in the school by our house, concluding that it would be a safer and better environment for him.

I now realized the difference that home environment had played in my nephew's life. Since my husband and I had joint custody with Peggy, we were always included on the emergency contact list for my niece and nephew. Prior to my nephew coming to live with us, I had been getting phone calls from one of his teachers informing me that he was being disruptive and wasn't listening in class. Subsequently I would ask Peggy why my nephew was acting out in class, to which she would respond, "I don't even know." Although she knew darn well why he was demonstrating such unruly behavior, she always claimed ignorance. But when he lived with us for two weeks, it was clear to us that something was happening at my sister's house that was causing him to act in this manner. He had only been with us for about three days when I received another phone call from Sammuelle's teacher, only this time she informed me that my nephew's behavior had improved significantly.

"He's now living with us temporarily," I told the teacher, "because of his mom's hospitalization."

"I knew something had to be different," the teacher responded, "because he is like a completely different child now." It was then that I realized that my nephew was not happy at home. Something was going on besides his mother's illness.

As I mentioned previously, Peggy's husband was an abusive man who had not only given her HIV but also resorted to violence against both her and my nephew. It wasn't until sometime later that I would find this out. As is the case with most battered women, each time that either I or Mama would ask Peggy about various suspicious episodes at her house, she would always deny what was really going on. When Mama would show up at her house unannounced, trying to help, Peggy would lash out at her with disrespect.

"You always in my business," Peggy would yell. "Why you comin' over here? Stay out of my business!"

But Mama still continued her surprise visits because, as she would always say to me, "Somethin' just ain't right."

Whenever my niece and nephew went to Mama's house, she would often question my nephew about things relative to either Peggy or her husband. If she asked him a question that he knew he would be punished for later if he told the truth, he would just put his head down and say, "I don't know," as he never wanted to lie to her. Sometime later however, we found out -- by pure accident, mind you -- that Peggy's husband had beaten Sammuelle like a slave who had unsuccessfully escaped from his master. One evening Mama went into Sammuelle's room while he was changing his shirt and was shocked when she saw huge, swollen welts on his back. When she asked him how he had gotten those, he told her that they apparently had appeared a few days after Peggy's husband had disciplined him.

Mama was devastated. She couldn't believe that someone would actually abuse a harmless 11- or 12-year-old child.

Lesson XII: *Life is about helping and encouraging others to reach their fullest potential.*

It's funny how, when you're experiencing turbulence in your life, you try not to even think about your situation (at least that's what I do). All I could do was just focus on the moment and take each day one step at a time. If I dwelled on my difficulties, I would find it hard to move past them, because all of my energy would go towards them and they would only get bigger. And so it was that I didn't pay much attention to the fact that now and then, I felt depressed. It was just one of those things that I had to move past. I'd try to shake off the feeling, and go on.

Needless to say, I had one goal in mind, and that was to successfully make it through the trimester, and pass my class with a "B" or better. Since I was able to make my own schedule for work, I scheduled my inspections as much as I could around my daughter's school hours, my class hours, and utilized the night hours to finish up my reports. This allowed me to always get my work done effectively, and still maintain my position as one of the top producers in my office.

Of course none of this would have been possible had it not been for my husband Daniel, and later on my mother as well. On most school nights my husband was always there to care for our daughter, unless there were times when he had to work late. On rare occasions, I was blessed to also have my mother willing and able to watch our daughter. On the nights I had class, Daniel would always make sure he was available to pick our daughter up from school. In addition, he also cared for my nephew for the brief time that he stayed with us when Peggy was hospitalized. I cannot honestly say how many husbands would be willing to watch not only their own child, but also their wife's nephew. Not once did I ever have to miss any of my classes or group meetings.

Class was sometimes challenging, because I was frequently the only African-American in the class. Whenever I wasn't the only African-American, the few others that were in class knew each other from prior classes and therefore would always formulate their groups with those persons whom they were familiar with, African-American or not. The feelings of isolation that I sometimes felt had more to do with the insecurities and shyness that I was developing over the course of my appraisal career, than with my classmates. Possibly they were linked to my bouts of depression as well.

In business you must definitely learn to be assertive, know how to network and make friends because this is what it takes to be successful. In my younger years growing up, I was quite comfortable talking to anyone, making speeches, and being in any situation where I had to "think on my feet." As I entered the appraisal arena, however, I had very few opportunities to perform such tasks. So as with anything else, as the saying goes "If you don't use it, you'll lose it."

Of course I could have attempted to maintain my speaking abilities, but as a wife, mother and busy professional, I found it hard to find the time to participate in such extracurricular activities. Needless to say, my natural speaking abilities deteriorated as long as I continued to not utilize them.

Chapter 17

AIDS and Willpower

There is nothing worse than lying in a hospital bed in a room alone with no one coming to visit you. My mother saw to it that this never happened to Peggy.

In my mind, it seemed as though every time a new trimester began, Peggy would go into the hospital. This was very discouraging for me because I was trying to better myself with a higher education that would ultimately improve my family's well-being, only to have it interrupted by unforeseen circumstances and responsibilities beyond those of my immediate family. Was it selfish of me to think this way? Now, in hindsight, I would venture to say yes. This was all about ego. Who cared whether or not I got that MBA or not? What matters most is being there for the people you care about, and having them know that they are important in your life -- that you will be there for them during their times of need.

When my sister first became ill to the point where she had to frequent the hospital often, I would just go without even thinking about it. However as time passed and Peggy refused to take her medication, I found it hard to go and visit knowing that the reason she was there was not because of her condition, but mainly because she wouldn't stick to her treatment. Whenever I would ask her why, she would always reply, "I'm tired of taking medicine and going to the doctor."

"But this is what you have to do to live," I always told her. "If not for yourself, then for your children."

Since then, I've realized that you can't encourage someone to live for their young children when they have no desire to live for themselves. If you lack love for yourself, it is practically impossible to love anybody else. This is what it had come down to for Peggy. Each time she told me she was tired of living and no longer wanted to take her medicine, I would ask her "But what about your kids? Don't you want to see them graduate from high school? And don't you want to be there when your daughter starts her own family?"

"They have you and Mama," she answered.

I tried telling her that children always want their own mother -- that they would choose her any day, ill and all, over my mother and me. But Peggy still wouldn't hear it. She continued to take her medication only sporadically, getting stronger whenever her husband was around. During these times she would take her medicine regularly, and then get weaker whenever he was no longer in her life, and she had stopped the medication. Her mind was telling her that she wasn't worthy of the task. She had allowed her soul to be tormented by her husband for such a long while that she felt she was not worthy of living.

One night I got a phone call late at night, around 1 or 2 a.m. Peggy was on the other end of the phone. "Veronica, I'm scared," she said to me.

"Why?" I asked her.

"I'm just scared. I had this strange feeling come over me."

"Do you still want to die?" I asked her.

"No, I don't want to die."

At that moment, I was so happy. Hearing my sister say that she no longer wanted to die was like I had just drank some non-decaffeinated coffee – straight, no cream just all caffeine (although I don't even drink coffee!). Those words were truly music to my soul. I then asked her if she wanted me to pray with her over the phone, and she said yes. So I did. To this very day, I don't know what made my sister call me that night, but I am so honored that she did. Whatever it was that brought her to do so, created a permanent, personal moment in time that allowed me to commune with God on her behalf. This was something that she had always previously refused to let anyone do, according to Mama.

Over the next few years, Peggy's condition continued to worsen until she could no longer take care of herself. Given the options of spending the rest of her days at an assisted-living facility or at her home, Peggy chose to live at home. My mother thought it best that Peggy lived with her so that she could be her caregiver. During that final year, after it was determined that Peggy's days were not long, Mama nursed her, bathed her and did everything a mother could do for her dying child. If my mother could have breathed for her, she would have.

It was now the summer of 2002, and time for me to enroll in my MBA classes for the fall. Initially I enrolled; however, soon after that, something was telling me that maybe I should take the fall trimester off since it looked like it was going to be quite challenging; School was resuming for Neemah, and Peggy's terminal condition. I decided that it would be best to take a break from graduate school.

I'm glad that I listened to that inner voice, because On October 27, 2002, which happened to be my sister Tanya's birthday, Peggy passed away.

It was a Saturday morning and Peggy's son, Sammuelle, was spending the weekend with us, when my mom called and told me that Peggy was now gone. I remember going into the bedroom where my nephew was sleeping, waking him up and breaking the news to him.

"Are you okay?" I asked him as I gave him a hug.

"Yes," he said, with a tear welling up.

I told him we would give him privacy to express his sadness.

Peggy's daughter, Karla, had spent the same weekend at my mother's and unfortunately had to see and experience her mom's final dying throes. Peggy had appeared to be fighting her transition to the other side. With my mom hovering beside her, she moaned as if to be in great pain and agony, until she took her final breath and transcended from this Earth. I cannot even imagine being a 10-year-old child and having to witness my mother's final suffering and death. Not until writing this book did I realize how detrimental and emotionally traumatic this must have been for Karla.

When you lose a loved one, there are so many things to get done that you oftentimes don't have time to think clearly. I was so concerned with making the funeral arrangements, and taking care of other business, that I didn't have time (or take the time) to think deeply about the additional support that both Karla and Sammuelle would need from this moment on.

Many African-Americans don't even entertain the idea of going to therapy, although this was undeniably something that Karla would need for a good portion of the remainder of her life. If you are experiencing a similar situation in your life, I would encourage you to seek therapeutic support for any children who have lost a parent or caregiver. Without question, the therapy will provide an outside resource to which the child can open up. When we are very young, we don't always want to confide in those who are close to us; it is sometimes preferable to indulge ourselves in conversation with a perfect stranger whose trust we have gained.

Chapter 18

Life After Someone Else's Death

For the first few weeks after Peggy's death, Sammuelle and Karla had continued to live in Lynwood with my brother, who had been caring for them during the final six months of Peggy's illness. Because Peggy was on government-assisted living (welfare) and she was now deceased, my brother and the kids had to give up the apartment. They then moved in with my mother in Los Angeles until we were able to sort things out.

Daniel and I decided that it would be best if the kids remained with my mother. But since Karla and Sammuelle were now our responsibility, we were concerned about their safety, and that of my mother. The Los Angeles neighborhood where I had grown up, where my mom currently lived was no longer the neighborhood that I had known. Well-maintained lawns, corner store and gas station, and friendly neighbors were no longer the norm. Instead the streets were dreary with poorly maintained lawns, and an abandoned gas station and corner store that were sometimes used as a dumping ground for old furniture and junk. Few of the remaining neighbors were people whom we had known.

One Friday night back in 1999, we were taking my Mom home after attending a program at Neemah's school. The time was about 9:30-10:00 p.m. When we reached my Mom's street, a police car blocked it. The officer told us that they were looking for someone involved in a shooting. Even though my Mom lived down that street, we wouldn't be able to enter until after the person was apprehended or was thought to no longer be in the immediate vicinity. Needless to say, my mother had to spend the night at our house because we didn't know how long it would be before they found who they were looking for. It was events such as this one that prompted us to want other living arrangements for my Mom, niece and nephew.

After Peggy's death, I took not only the fall trimester off, but several following trimesters as well. Inevitably Pepperdine University sent me a letter saying that, due to my extended absence, they were withdrawing me from the program.

The school's action didn't devastate me, however. I had a great task ahead in caring for not only my immediate family but also my niece and nephew. As we discussed what was best for the kids, Daniel felt that it would be the best idea to move them and my Mom out of Los Angeles. So we purchased another home for ourselves, and moved my mother, Karla and Sammuelle into our old home, just outside of Los Angeles.

By God's grace (and also because of Daddy's financial lessons), Daniel and I were able to support these two households because we had always managed to live below our means. I had been driving the same 1990 Honda Civic (which was Daniel's car when we first met) for work for the last 2 years, and Daniel continued to drive our

1995 Volvo station wagon. If we had previously decided to buy a bigger and better home (since we had owned our first home for about 5 years), along with two new fancy cars, we more than likely would not have been able to afford this opportunity for my Mom, my niece and nephew.

After we settled the three of them into their new community, we enrolled the kids in their new schools, which were conveniently located nearby. Daniel and I strongly believed that this would hopefully give Sammuelle and Karla a new beginning and the opportunity to have some stability in their lives.

My sister's death made me think deeply about how a person can fight the feelings that swallowed her will to live. In hindsight, I now realize that my sister undoubtedly demonstrated signs of depression. As I will discuss later, when depression sets in, your desire to live is diminished significantly.

What I also learned was this: If you find yourself in a situation where you have given up on life, change something in your daily routine. Instead of watching your favorite television show, go out for a walk or do some exercises. This will encourage the creative energies that are probably lying dormant inside of you and are waiting to be activated. Stop thinking about your situation, and turn your thoughts to how you would like your life to be at this moment. Fantasize about how this particular moment could be made perfect. As much as possible, imagine your perfect moment from your perspective, thinking about what you would change about yourself right now, that could make you happier. The point here is to only focus on you and any positive changes that you desire for yourself which will cause you to feel good about who you are.

Also utilize the positive affirmations that were discussed earlier. The more positive thoughts and words you inundate your mind and psyche with, the better you will feel. Recite to yourself, "My future is bright, and I am Blessed by the Almighty God." Say this to yourself several times during the day, especially when you are feeling down. This will cause your subconscious mind to put events in motion that will bring truth to these statements. Do not succumb to the evils of depression and self-doubt, especially if you are a mother. You can overcome these emotional states if you truly believe that you can. Again, believe it and you will achieve it!

Lesson XIII: *Motherhood and womanhood are responsibilities that shape the future for a lifetime.*

We need all mothers to be strong for their children, and to feel good about who they are. A mother who feels good about herself will raise children who feel good about who they are. Mothers with a positive self-image can raise children with a positive self-image. A strong mother will raise her children with an unspoken love and strength that cannot be taken away. A strong mother raises children who grow up to be good leaders. In other words, the strength of the future is in the hands of all mothers.

If you are a mother, you have the power to manipulate the future, whether you know it or not. If you have a low self-image, you will unfortunately allow your children to be raised with a similar self-image. Your children will therefore be easily manipulated by the world. Children with a low self-image allow others to abuse them, or grow up to be abusive, simply because they are looking for love and for someone to accept them. The truth of the matter is -- since they have no self-love -- the people whom they attract into their lives will love them with that same amount of love...none. If you love yourself a little, you will attract people into your life that will only love you a little.

If you love yourself a lot, you will attract people into your life that love you even more. Love who you are and focus on what's good and positive in your life, and you will see a change in your life. Love yourself with an abundance of love, like a bouquet of flowers, and you will love your children with this same amount of love or even more.

What I am saying here is not to diminish or belittle the role of fatherhood, but to magnify every woman's self-image. This way, she can attract the best father figure for her children if no such person exists currently in her life. A woman who feels good about *who* she is, not what she is (doctor, lawyer, teacher, etc), will find the best man for her and her future, because this is the energy that she not only generates but projects. In turn, this energy will capture the attention of only those men who also want this woman to continue to ignite such energy. If he's a smart man, he will know that a woman with such an energy will only be a blessing and strong foundation for his home.

In order to have a positive impact on the future, we as women must first love who we are. As we love ourselves, this is a demonstration of our love for God. When I speak of loving yourself, I'm not speaking of vanity. Instead, what I am referring to is an acceptance of who you are—your past, who your parents are or were, how you grew up. Everything about your life has to be accepted by you in order for others to accept you. This is a prerequisite if you want to move your life forward with confidence. Show me someone who doesn't love themselves, and I will show you a person who is either lonely or surrounded by other people who really don't like that person either.

Right now, there is probably someone sitting with this book right now, saying, "But, Veronica, how can I love myself when I've done some terrible things in my life?" Or, "How can I love who I am when my mother (or father) is or was a drug addict?" "How can I love myself when I've never done anything significant in my life?" And I could go on and on with questions like this, because I'm sure you are thinking of some reasons right now as you read these words. "How can I love myself when I've been a bad mother by neglecting my children?"

I am here to tell you that those reasons don't matter. None of them matter. What matters most is this moment right now. This is the moment that your life will change because now /today you will stop thinking about what you are not, or what you don't have, and all the negative aspects of your life. Instead, you will focus your energies on that which is positive in your life. And I don't want to hear that there's nothing positive in your life. If you are an American or are living in America at this moment, the simple fact that you live here in America is a blessing unto itself. You could be living in other parts of the World, where you don't know whether you are going to live or die tomorrow or in the next minute.

The concept of self-love sounds very easy, but rest assured that, although it should come fairly easy, this is sometimes hard for people to do. I'll give you some examples of this. Do you think a woman who prostitutes herself has a genuinely strong sense of self-worth? It's doubtful that she does. Somewhere along her life's path, she was probably subjected to some form of abuse and neglect, which led her to a life of prostitution. This life that she leads does not make her any less of a person than any of us; however, it more than likely does cause her to feel as though she is not a worthy person. What about the man who abuses his wife? Does he have a strong self-image? More than likely, the answer is no.

You see, the more you love who you are, the more you love God. God made us in His own image, so as you cherish the person that God made you to be, you are actually demonstrating your appreciation to God for His gift of life to you. If you have a low self-image or low self-esteem (which are one in the same), you ultimately have a very low level of love for God. You can't tell me that you love God, but not yourself. This is pretty much impossible because you are a reflection of God. God, our source of life, lives inside each and every one of us. The more we realize and recognize this, the stronger we become as a person.

How is it that you expect others to believe in you despite your past, yet you won't allow yourself to move beyond some events of your past because you consistently still revisit them? Don't expect others to do things for you that in truth, you will not do for yourself. For you to be successful, you must first commit to overcoming the challenges that are guaranteed to meet you along the way. Many of us have a tendency to blame others for our past pitfalls and misfortunes without first taking a step back and seeing how we may have contributed to these events.

Always investigate the past by stepping outside yourself and reviewing the events as if you were watching a movie. In this way, you will most likely have a more objective view of what actually occurred. Not only can you see it from a different perspective, but you can also remove yourself from the situation, preventing yourself from personalizing any attacks that may have been launched at you. If you do this, you will probably have a better understanding of the reasons as to why certain events transpired. How wonderful is that?

We all are stars in movies about our own lives, if we can only see ourselves that way. Many events will have completely different outcomes once we know that we have the power to re-write the script.

Remember, it is always better to be victorious than a Victim. In every challenging situation, I want you to think about this question: What type of "Vic" are you? I want you to invariably choose to be a Victor and not a Victim. Victims are the result of circumstances, while Victors are the winners of change, because with every circumstance comes some form of mutation. At every opportune moment, choose to be victorious in your own right, by defining what victory means to you. We all are different with varying levels of talent and tastes, so why should we all be defined by the same attitudes? My mental capacity is not the same as yours, and yours is not the same as the next person's. So why do we allow ourselves to be judged based on goals and aspirations that do not apply to our personal lives? We must refrain from doing so.

Many of us are born leaders, and when we're younger, we know this about ourselves and act upon it accordingly. But as we get older, we give in to the criticisms and expectations of others instead of continuing to *know* who we are and recognize our full potential. Our full potential usually lies outside of what others/society have dictated for us. From our moment of birth, we are all destined for greatness; in order to fulfill that destiny, we must chart our own course. If we allow someone else to determine our course, we could end up anywhere -- or worse, we could end up nowhere.

Each of us is born with purpose; it is our lifetime duty to figure out our purposes while here on Earth. We must not allow the world to determine our purposes for us, just as we cannot allow society and the world at large to define what success is to us. Once you have firmly decided what success means to you, not only will it be the appropriate challenge for you, but you will also find it more profound, applicable and meaningful to your life. In turn, your decision will accent the lives of those around you. Be well, and think well, and with God's help, follow your heart's content to your destinies. For this is the stuff that you and I, as true human spirits, are made of.

Lesson XIV: *"We become what we think about." --Earl Nightingale*

The moment you change your thinking is the moment your life will change. See the World as beautiful and you will experience beauty every day. If however, you see the World as a cold and cruel place, you will experience coldness and cruelty in your life adventures. As Dr. Wayne Dyer says in his book, *The Power of Intention*, "If you change the way you look at things, the things that you look at will change." For example, you may think, "Oh I'm stupid" or "...I can't make it in this world because it's just too hard." If this is how you think, then guess what, you will live your life each day as though you had no common sense. Or if you think the latter, you will experience life as an endless struggle.

We as humans have unfortunately been conditioned to jump right to the negative aspect(s) whenever something happens. For example, if you have a car accident, whether it is your fault or not, the first thing you might think about is, "Aw, man, I have messed up my car!" or "He has messed up my car!"

As a demonstration of how this works, I have quite the example to share with you. There's a colleague and friend of mine who, while raising her nephew, decided to buy him a car after he turned 16 since he was a fairly decent kid with academic honors. She also commenced to incur the expense because having his own transportation would also give him the freedom and responsibility of being able to provide his own way to school and other places in which he desired to go.

Well, one day he had an accident in the car, and she called me quite upset of course because her nephew had hit someone. She was really frantic because once the insurance company was made aware of the accident, her premium would more than likely get increased. She therefore wanted to have the car repaired without reporting the incident to the insurance company.

I stopped her in the midst of her venting and asked, "Was your nephew hurt? Was anyone else hurt?"

"No," she said. "No one was hurt. And the car can be fixed."

I then shared with her that first of all, we should thank God that no one was hurt because that in itself could have brought its own stress, depending on the seriousness of the injuries involved. Secondly, I told her to thank God that she had the ability to pay for the car to even get repaired, and also that the car was insured to begin with. So this was not the worst that it could have been. After I asked her these questions, which helped her to change her thoughts about the accident, she then told me "You know what? Hey, I guess you're right. It could have been much worse so I guess I'd better stop my complaining."

In a situation such as this, we must focus on the positive, start thinking about the solution so that we can move forward, and see the lesson that this accident presents. There's always a lesson to be learned in every situation, especially when the situation involves a teenage driver!

When our daughter first began kindergarten at the age of 4 and was learning how to do simple mathematics such as addition and subtraction, she would sometimes become frustrated and say how hard the work was. I would respond by telling her, "Stop staying that it's hard. Say, 'It's challenging but I can do it." This same logic applies to life. Life is not hard. Although it might be quite challenging, guess what? You can make it! So instead of saying, "Life is hard", from this moment forward, always know and believe this: "Life is challenging, but I can make it." Make this your mantra whenever you start to experience any obstacles or difficulties. Truly, life is all in how you look at it.

I like that KCET log line that they often air between some of the shows. A child's voice says, "It's all in how you look at it." This is true of everything in life. There is something positive in every situation, but you must sometimes seek it out, especially when something bad happens.

My point with all of this is that we must change the way we think from day to day if we want to be more "Christ-like," or more like God. Let's go from a "welfare" mentality to a "wealth" mentality. I ask you, can you see God walking around saying, "...Oh, what a mess I have made." Or, "...Oh, I am just useless!" No! Absolutely not. Think on the World through God's eyes. If we see the World and ourselves as God sees us, we will experience life as we never have before.

Chapter 19

Time to Move On to A New Adventure

Lesson XV: *Life is about sacrifices.*

Over the years, through a good part of my adult life, the sacrifices I've been called on to make have taught me a great deal about their importance. My husband has made them as well.

For example -- as a wife, mother, and exemplary employee, I sacrificed my sleep time in order that I could do an excellent job at work (working 12 hours or more per day), and still manage to be there for my husband and daughter, and be the best wife and mom I could possibly be. I would literally sleep an average of only four hours per night, which is probably quite normal for many working mothers and wives.

A typical day would start at about 6:00 a.m. I would wake up, shower and make breakfast for my family. After we were dressed and ready for the day, I would take our daughter to school and then set out for my workday. In the afternoon, when school was out, I would pick up our daughter from the bus stop or school, and then we would head home. As she completed her homework I would work on my reports for work (I worked mostly from home), taking breaks as needed to assist Neemah with homework questions.

At about 5 p.m. I would pause my workday to prepare dinner, and then start the workday again at about 8:30 or 9 p.m. after Neemah had been put to bed.

Now I don't know whether you've noticed or not, but there wasn't any mention here about time (other than dinner) that I would spend with my husband. This is because, for about eight out of the first ten years of our marriage, my husband (not always willingly of course) had to live with me working constantly day and night. There was never much time for husband-and-wife moments during the week. I don't know many men who would put up with this, but he did. It was a sacrifice that he made. For years Daniel would often encourage me to come to bed and stop working so late until eventually he gave up.

Because I worked solely on commission (i.e. if I didn't obtain a certain set amount in monthly charges and only produced enough to receive the minimum salary, more than likely I would eventually get laid off), I felt that I didn't have a choice. Of course the money was good, and in the beginning of my career as a real-estate appraiser my job wasn't as demanding.

After several years, however, my employer merged with another big bank, and the requirements got even more stringent. Now I had to work seven days a week on a 24-hours-a-day clock. Eventually my husband started telling me, "I don't care about the money. You only have one you. If you dropped dead tomorrow, that bank is going to continue on without you."

I was working not only for my immediate family, but also for my mother, and my niece and nephew. As long as I worked hard, they would always have a nice place to call home. On the other hand, I knew I couldn't carry on indefinitely like this, working long hours and not spending quality time with my family.

So the moment came when I changed my thinking about work. I decided to move on from my "parent company" so that I could be at peace and my family could be at peace as well. I had worked there since age 15, so now I prayed and meditated that God would help me to find a new company that valued its employees.

Shortly after this time, a smaller bank offered me a position. Going by my research and interviews, I felt that this company cared about their employees and would not require the long hours that I was previously working. In addition, they told me that my income would be comparable to that at my parent company. Hearing this, I knew I had nothing to lose.

Obviously my time at my parent company was over. My purpose for being there had been fulfilled and a new appointment awaited me. However, if I concentrated only on how comfortable I was at my parent company, and how my current work situation was demolishing my life, things would only get even more chaotic. More than likely my life wasn't ruined yet, but it would get that way if this were what I focused my thoughts and energy on.

I definitely wanted to leave the company on a positive note, for it truly had been the best company I had ever worked for, and my strongest desire was to always remember it in this way. My parent company had contributed to my success by allowing me several opportunities to move up within the company. It was my 19 years there that helped me to become successful and financially wealthy.

This is how I wanted to remember the company that had been a major part of not only my life but my family's lives as well.

With only a one-day break in between, I left my parent company and went on to a new adventure at a new bank.

The beginning was just wonderful. I felt as though I should have been there a long time ago. What had taken me so long to get to a company that appeared to value their employees? Put simply, comfort had kept me from change, which ultimately leaves you open to the unknown. Most of us prefer suffering through our current jobs since we prefer the pros and cons to making a change that, in our minds, may or may not be beneficial to our growth and well- being.

Six months into my new job I was still quite happy.

By this time I was moved to a different appraisal office and a new manager. The new placement actually put me closer to home, so I was ecstatic about that. My new manager had very little appraisal experience so I was there to add my years of experience and knowledge to the mostly novice staff of appraisers. It was truly enjoyable for me to share my knowledge with this new staff, and the manager was quite content that I had been sent to this office -- at least, so it seemed.

During my first week at the new office, I did notice that the atmosphere here was different from that of the prior office. There just wasn't the same positive energy that I had felt earlier. After working there for about a week, I realized that this was going to be a different experience --not necessarily bad, just different. After about a few months I had grown accustomed to the environment and was once again starting to feel good again. The manager and I spoke about my acting as his assistant in his absence since this was also a condition of my new assignment -- to gain managerial experience.

Almost a year after I went to this new company, I suddenly found myself feeling depressed again, except this time it was more frequently and for longer periods of time.

It was hard to figure out what was wrong with me. I had no desire to get up and go to work. When I pulled into the parking lot at my office building, I would sit in my car for about 15 minutes. I had to pray and ask God to give me the strength to go into the office and be happy or at least content, not showing others the agony that I was experiencing because it had nothing to do with them. I did not want to treat others in my office sorely just because I was having a bad week.

Finally, since this job offered a little flexibility, I decided to work from home. There was no need to go into the office feeling depressed day after day. To do so would surely come close to an act of punishment towards myself.

After some time had passed while being at my new office, I started sending out weekly Motivational Quotes that I would collect from Nightingale-Conant and other inspirational authors. One day, my manager came out of his office to converse with me and the one other appraiser who was there at the time. After the conversation had been going for a short while, he proceeded to tell us how some time ago his grandmother would email a daily prayer to him and all of his family members.

"I told her not to send any more of those emails to me," the manager went on, "because I can't get that type of stuff at work." He then jokingly (with a chuckle) asked me, "Are *you* going to start sending out daily prayers next?"

It was only about two or three weeks prior that I had sent out the first quote, yet he was already making it a point to let me know how he felt about them. I found it amazing that certain people reject positive gestures, while they warmly welcome non-positive emails that ridicule others -- to the point where it almost seemed to place joy in their hearts when they read an email that belittled another.

After this encounter and other comments, that revealed the manager's true character, I truly began to feel out of place.

My husband had always told me that in any company, the culture is typically top-down. If you're in a department where the manager is unhappy with his personal or professional life and unashamedly reveals his lack of happiness by his or her behavior around other employees, more than likely you will find that his staff is usually less content as well. Constant complaining by staff members, lack of enthusiasm for the job, and/or very little respect for management, are sometimes a demonstration of this. Oftentimes you will even find people sharing secrets about the manager. Such work environments result in a lack of productivity and stunted growth.

Managers must therefore exercise great care in the manner in which they interact with staff members, both at the office and at offsite events. The language of the Miranda Law states clearly that "anything you say can and will be used against you." The same principle can apply in your everyday workplace, where character – or the lack of it -- definitely applies.

Chapter 20

The Work/Career "Life Cycle"

From the experience mentioned in the previous chapter, I realized that, just as products have a "life cycle," so do employees.   It was to be one of the most important lessons for me in the business world.

The marketing life cycle of a product typically involves four stages: the Introductory stage—Growth stage—Maturity stage—Declining stage. The introductory stage is exactly that. This is the period when the product is first introduced to the market; there is great enthusiasm from the market about the product. In the second phase, the product is well known and demand is high (growing) to the point of full maturity, hence the third stage. In the maturity stage, the product manages to net the most profits, although growth tends to be at a slower pace. After demand has maximized, you will find that the market is no longer excited (enthusiasm is diminished) about the product because something better has come along. It then enters the fourth stage—which is the declining period.

This same concept applies to each employee. However, instead of Introductory-Growth-Maturity and Decline, the four stages of the employee life cycle are Enthusiastic stage—Challenging/Learning stage—Growing stage—Declining stage. When an employee starts a new position, there is a great deal of enthusiasm involved. He or she is very excited about the new assignment and is off to a rushing start, setting out to be the best in the business. In this stage, negative comments or scenarios have no basis and warrant no reaction from the employee because they are on a career high.

In the second phase, the employee is being challenged in various ways because she is learning the business or tasks. Whenever there are challenges, there is a great deal of learning taking place. These challenges might be daily, weekly or monthly; however in each case, there will be some degree of learning implicated. At this point, the employee feels a sense of accomplishment and admiration because of the level of knowledge intake, which leads into the next stage.

In the third phase or growth stage, similar to a product, the employee is now well known because of her ability. As a result, she is recognized and possibly rewarded -- not only because of growth, but also because of the contributions to the company. It is in the growth stage that the employee is at the top of her game and others come to her for assistance and advice in perfecting their jobs, because they want to know how she was able to do it. What is it that allowed her to arrive at this point? These are some of the questions that fellow co-workers will ask or demonstrate in their desire to replicate the successful employee's behaviors and methodologies.

Once the high has worn off, the employee has now entered the fourth stage.

Here, she or he encounters some challenges but none that require much effort to overcome. Unlike the third stage, where there is substantial and continuous growth, the decline stage is more or less the opposite with growth being stunted. The employee feels that he is no longer making an impact in the department and organization. He doesn't have the desire to do so because the position doesn't present notable challenges. Learning has ceased, and growth is now virtually non-existent.

I strongly believe in the quote, "Learning is wealth," which I was fortunate to encounter at the Long Beach Museum of Art in Long Beach, California during an exhibit titled "Portraits of a People: Picturing African Americans in the Nineteenth Century." This quote is incredibly true and powerful. As in the case of the employee in the Decline stage of the life cycle, if your mind is not being stimulated in some way, you are being robbed of great riches. To learn is to build internal and external wealth. You can only go as far as you are willing to learn new things.

Learning is one of those gifts of life that's priceless. The more you know, the more you grow; and the more you grow, the better you feel about who you are and who you've come to be. I view learning in the same way that I view giving: the day you stop learning is the day you die. The day that I can no longer give is the day that I can no longer live. Living is learning, and giving is living.

If you find yourself in the fourth stage of the employee life cycle, chances are that it's time for a change that will benefit not only you but your company as well. Whether you change positions internally or externally, the need to do so is there. You not only benefit yourself when you move on to something more challenging, you also benefit your organization by allowing someone else to fill in where you have left off. Your replacement will now embark upon the journey that you just traveled, and you will begin a new path where the life cycle will be repeated.

Chapter 21

Obtaining Work/Life Balance

One evening while attending a Pepperdine Alumni event, I was engaged in conversation with two young gentlemen whom I had just met. They worked at Ameriprise. We were discussing our tenure at our companies.

"One of the reasons I left my parent company," I told the young men, "was because it was pretty much the only company I had ever worked for. I wanted to get a different experience from another financial-services institution."

One of the gentlemen, whom we will call Victor, had a different view. "I've worked for my company for just over 10 years," he said. "I began working there right out of college, and I just couldn't imagine working anywhere else."

Clearly Victor had a lot of enthusiasm and love for his company. He went on to tell me, "My brother has worked for Ameriprise too, for about the same amount of time. And he has the same feelings as me regarding the company."

But Victor had overlooked the fact that I had worked for my parent company for almost twice as long as he had been at Ameriprise, so our feelings and experiences would definitely be very different from one another.

In addition, the young men didn't appear to understand that the corporate experience for a female is much more challenging than it is for males. When it comes to roles in the family, a female professional who is married with children has significantly more responsibilities than does a male with a similar familial status.

During that conversation, I also shared with Victor and Michael that when you're at a large corporation, you often endure the inevitable merger experience. Depending on which company is in the "acquiring" position, will ultimately determine what the culture and management style of the newly formed larger institution will be. Prior to my departure from my Parent Bank we had previously merged with another lending institution in which, unlike many of the past mergers, Parent Bank was not in the "acquiring" position. Needless to say, the new corporate culture saw some drastic changes.

Among other things, the Appraisal Department had been confronted with new requirements, including a 7-days-a-week cycle time which meant that weekends were not only being included in our "expected days of completion" but we would also start receiving work around the clock, 24 hours 7 days a week, holidays included. Of course these new requirements had been met with opposition from the staff appraisers who were now beginning to feel that their lives were being taken away. Regardless of whether you spoke to an appraiser in Tennessee or California, virtually every appraiser felt the same way about these requirements -- that he or she couldn't "have a life" because of working 7 days a week to meet these new expectations.

After years of staying up until 2 a.m. each night (which was true for most of the appraisers in my office) attempting to meet this new demand, I gave my manager my letter of resignation. Upon receiving it she repeatedly asked me to stay and inquired about what could be done to make me change my mind. Apparently her manager had told her that they needed to do whatever it took to maintain the top producers. "I consider you as one of those top producers," she said.

I conveyed to her that one of the new requirements would need to be changed.

"That can't be done," my manager said.

"Then could we get our weekends and holidays back, and not have them included in our cycle time?" I pursued.

"No, that can't be done either," my manager emphasized sadly.

"Then I have to leave," I had said. "Because under the current conditions and requirements, I can't spend any quality time with my family."

From my conversation with the young gentlemen at Pepperdine, I could see that they had not yet lived through such a corporate challenge.

I still enjoyed being both a working mother and wife. However there had to be a balance between the two. In order for me to do a successful job at work, I have to know that I am also being a successful mother and wife, regardless of the amount of money that I am earning. If this is not the case, my work will suffer. While working all those excessive, unappreciated hours, my thoughts would continue to divert to the fact that I was laboriously meeting the demands of work but unable to spend even an hour at the park with my daughter and husband during the week.

The company where I was now working did not make any of the excessive demands that my prior company had. Yet at this moment, because of the other developing circumstances that I've mentioned, it became clear to me that I had to make changes in my life for my family's sake. At the end of the day, when all of the work is done and my life is at its end, as a mother, wife, daughter, aunt, and sister, it will not be the professional work I did which I will value the most. It will surely be the time that I spent with my family.

It is an unfortunate fact of the business world that companies fail to realize how much better off they would be if they helped their employees to have a work/life balance. I would highly recommend that companies not deprive their employees of time to spend with their families.

To illustrate, I will share an incident that I was unfortunately able to witness. One day while I was picking up my daughter from child care, I passed a mother and her daughter as they were leaving the building. The daughter was explaining to her mother how she didn't have all the materials needed for her sewing class. The mother was fairly agitated and told her daughter, "I don't have time to get those supplies today. And I'm fed up with this facility not being as organized as they should be."

That mother may have suffered from stress on the job due to the requirements and restrictions placed upon her by her employer. Let's imagine this mother in a different scenario. This time around, the mother has a pleasant day at work, with enough time to complete all of her critical tasks, in addition to being able to plan out the following day, including her less critical tasks. Because she has completed all of her work in a timely fashion, she is able to help other employees get their jobs done more efficiently. At the end of the day, when she picks her daughter up from child care and the little lady tells her about the needs for sewing class, the mother happily responds, "Would you like to go and get those supplies today?"

Her daughter smiles, takes her mother's hand and replies, "Oh yes, thank you, Mommy!"

These are two very different outcomes, involving the same people, same setting, but completely different circumstances prefacing the visit to the childcare. How wonderful life would be for many of us, if our working lives were mostly pleasant and fulfilling to the point that we weren't required to sacrifice our home lives and personal time. The main point to remember here is that happy employees raise happy families. In addition, happy employees are much more productive employees.

Chapter 22

Deciding Which Way to Turn

Lesson XVI: *Always turn to your Spiritual Maker*

Today, as I write this book, I am experiencing Heaven on Earth. I say it this way because I know no other way to put it.

At this point in my life, I don't recall any other time where I've felt closer to God, my Heavenly and Earthly provider. This point in my life was a long road to travel, and progress did not come easily. But you know what? I wouldn't exchange the feeling that I feel right now for anything….not even a lifetime of riches, because this moment cannot be bought. This feeling that I am experiencing would bring peace in the Middle East, and peace to our most violent U.S. cities. If everyone reached this point in their lives, if they experienced this feeling, they would be the happiest people on earth. No, not one of the happiest persons but THE happiest person on Earth because what they would feel is something that can't be quantified.

This feeling and the experiences that brought me here, although hard and at times devastating, also brought me closer to God.

There were days where I just didn't want to get out of bed and go to work because I was so "work depressed." And when you're "work depressed," that feeling affects not only yourself but also everyone around you because your thoughts and words are sometimes quite negative. But the only way to get through something like that is to become grounded (if you are not already) in your spiritual relationship with God.

When the going gets rough, ultimately, you turn not to the television, not to your spouse, not to alcohol or drugs, not to your parent(s), not to friends…YOU TURN TO GOD. Whether you call him Buddha, Jehovah, Allah, Emmanuel, Jesus…whatever your name for Him really doesn't matter because there is only one God. The main message here is that during difficult times, you turn to your Source. I am a firm believer that no ONE religion is the right religion. What works for me may not work for you, and what works for you may not work for the next person. Turn to God to help you work through your difficulties because only you and your source (your higher spiritual self) can get you successfully through. However, you must have the willpower to make it through, and the faith that your spirit will be with you to get you past this distressing point in your life.

What happens when you turn to our Earthly co-occupants is that we don't get ALL of the answers we're looking for. We are still incomplete and ultimately still unhappy. You must resort to God or you will find yourself still searching for the right answers. I can honestly say that God has blessed me so much that I only go to HIM during times of distress. The people that are the closest to me can attest to this and tell you that when I'm going through a difficult time, I refrain from discussing it with them. The reason being that I just didn't believe that discussing it repeatedly with others would help the matter by any means.

During the time after my sister Peggy passed away, I was speaking with Tracy, a friend of mine, and she said, "It seems to me that nothing ever seems to bother you. No matter what you're going through, you always stay cool."

I didn't know it then, but my "cool" came from my Faith in God. As long as you have undisputed Faith, you have undisputed power over your life. Nothing and no one else besides you and God control your life. No matter what life throws at you, you can bounce right back stronger than before.

And what good would it do to worry and get stressed out over anything? Doing so will not help the situation. As a matter of fact, it only makes you feel worse and out of control of the matter. Always know that you and God are in control and he has your best interest. Regardless of what comes your way, you're going to deal with it because he gives you the power to do so.

For example, if I were to be laid off from my job, I wouldn't have freaked out. Fortunately this was something I'd learned from my phenomenal teachers Dr. Wayne Dyer and Deepak Chopra (whom I have never met personally, mind you). Instead of freaking out, I would embrace the lay-off as a new opportunity and adventure that God has chosen for my life. The path that I traveled would now be taking me in a new direction. I would now be turning down a different street. And what is down this street? I don't know. But I would be reassured because I know that God will be there for me, just as He has been in the past.

Life is a lot like driving. If you drive down the same street day after day after day, you don't get to see anything different. However, if you venture down an unfamiliar street, you are guaranteed to experience something new. Whether that something new is good or bad is all in how you choose to look at it. It's like that saying goes where, two people can look at the same picture and each of them see something different.

If I freak out about being laid off, it would mean that I didn't accept responsibility and move forward; instead, I would remain stagnant by only concentrating on the past. As Brian Tracy indicates in his audio series, *The Psychology of Achievement*, "When we accept responsibility, we look to the future and to what we can do. But when we blame, we look to the past and to what cannot be undone or changed. Responsibility looks forward and blame looks backward." To focus on the past means you aren't focusing on the future and the unlimited possibilities. So, by embracing this new opportunity, I would open myself up to the wonderful world that God had created for me to enjoy. If I focused only on the positive aspects of my new laid-off status, I will attract positive events into my life. But if I freak out and become bitter about my situation, I will only attract chaos and more misfortune into my life.

I don't know about you, but I prefer to look forward, not backward. This has been my way of dealing with life as I have come to know it.

Another reason why my girlfriends believed I wasn't bothered by difficult circumstances was because I don't publicize my problems. Since I didn't talk much about them, it meant I didn't give them power. The only power I gave them was the power to exist and nothing more.

When you reveal something negative in your life, and you keep on talking about it to others, you're only giving it power. The more you talk about it, the more power it obtains. So 90% of the time, I choose to talk about and focus on the positive. *This* is a Welfare to Wealth mentality.

So again I ask you, "What type of Vic are you? Are you a victim or a victor? Always choose to be a victor and not a victim. A victor is forever claiming victory over some sort of circumstance, while a victim wades in sorrow over a past wrong that cannot be undone. Additionally, a victim can never gather all the wealth that is out there to be gathered.

Chapter 23

We Can Make Life What We Want It To Be

After some time had passed, I was debating whether or not to return to graduate school. Some days the answer was yes, and others I just didn't want to even think about school, especially at this point in my life.

Once I was asked if I would trade my life in for a different one -- one that was more stable -- to which I would quickly reply, "Absolutely not!" What is a stable life? Every human that exists on this planet has to deal with something whether they come from a stable household or not. That's the beauty of life. We are all works in progress, because to live a perfect life would mean living a life without a need to learn. Learning is that part of life that makes it so grand.

As mentioned previously, one of my philosophies is that living is learning. If you're not learning something, you've mentally stopped living. To live is to learn and give. As you learn and give, others will benefit from your knowledge and understanding, for that is what makes life come full circle. For as you live, give and learn, someone is living, receiving and teaching; and the cycle will then repeat itself through infinity. We are all here with a purpose to fulfill. We are alive so therefore we are all living. Whether we're giving, learning, or teaching, it is these aspects of life that make it worth living. For as you teach, someone is learning; as someone learns, they are growing; as you give, someone is receiving and you too are receiving a positive energy that will bless you in return. So live to give, always thinking of ways in which you can help someone else. If you live your life in this manner, you shall always be blessed.

Lesson XVII: *See yourself not as someone in need, but someone with the power to help others.*

Regardless of your current situation right now, you have the power and opportunity to give to someone in need of assistance. You will be amazed at how good this will make you feel (not to mention how good the person on the receiving end will feel). It doesn't have to be something big or monetary. It could be the gift of your positive conversation or warm smile. The lyrics of India.Arie's song "There's Hope" tell us "It doesn't cost a thing to smile, you don't have to pay to laugh, you better thank God for that."

So be thankful and giving along life's path, and you will find yourself more blessed than you could ever imagine. Life is not about you, but what YOU can do for someone else. Be a giver, expecting nothing in return and life's door of abundance will be opened to you. The more you feel that you can give, the more you will be able to give. Expect nothing out of life, and you will receive nothing. Expect greatness, and not only will you become great, but you will receive the greater things in life.

Always focus on the positive aspects of your life and how blessed you are. Focus not on what you don't have or what you want, but on that which you have been so fortunate to receive already, because somewhere out in the world there exists someone who is in dire need of the very things you already own.

How dare we feel sorry for ourselves as if we are without! Without what? That bigger home, nicer car, fancier jewelry? For what? Now I'm not saying that you shouldn't want nice things in life, but do not make this your life mission. Set out to help someone or fill a need that will feel good to you. Whether that need is being a friend, an act of kindness, or giving someone that feeling of belonging. You never know, you could be just the person to fill that need.

Above all, do not doubt yourself and your worth. We are all priceless in the eyes of God. No one of us is better than the other, regardless of what we've done, good or bad. See yourself as not being better than someone, but just as good. Compare yourself to no one. For the only person that you can truly compare yourself to is you. The only person who has the same parents, upbringing, environment, talents, physical characteristics as you, is YOU! How unfortunate it is for us to compare ourselves to others who are nothing like us. We are truly putting ourselves at a disadvantage when we do this.

If you want to be better, then do better and be better than you did and were yesterday. Set goals for you! If there is something that you would like to accomplish, write out a plan as to how you will get there. See yourself completing that goal and know that you can do it.

After conversing with my husband and much deliberation, I came to that point in my story that I shared earlier -- the decision to return to Pepperdine University and finish my graduate studies at the Graziadio School of Business. There's nothing worse than starting something and never finishing it. I did not want to become another statistic of someone of African-American descent who might begin an endeavor, only to find that it's not a smooth road, and therefore call it quits, never to pursue it again. This had never been one of my modes of operation.

Because I'd been absent from school for quite some time and Pepperdine had withdrawn me from that program, I had to get permission from the University to re-enroll. So I wrote a letter and completed the necessary forms, and was granted re-admission. Thank goodness for the timing of my re-entry, because since my prior departure, Pepperdine had restructured the Fully Employed Graduate program, and now the requirements for graduation were slightly different than earlier. However, there were still a few classes that I could take from the old program structure, which would allow me to graduate in a timely manner and without having to endure additional classes.

A little over a year later, I graduated and received my Master's of Business Administration. As I said before, this was another milestone that I was able to reach mainly because of God's ever-present mercy and existence in my life. It was also made possible by the undying support of my husband. Not once did I have to worry about our daughter's safety or well-being because, on most days and evenings, she was in his care. I thank God and my husband for being the foundation that allows me to soar in my journey.

As spouses, we don't always recognize the support that we are given within our marriages, oftentimes until it is too late. Every relationship and marriage has its demons to fight, but let us not forget to enjoy and dwell upon the goodness and beauty of our connection to each other -- that beauty that brought us together in the first place. In this modern day and age of robust technology and advancements, we can get lost in our efforts to be the best husband or wife that we can possibly be. But our best is there, and in a marital union, it is our responsibility and duty to recognize that best in each other. Most of the time, we can only give what we were taught and what we have right now.

Again, the same philosophy applies here that was mentioned previously – the one about not comparing ourselves to others. We must not compare our spouses to the neighbor, or to our co-worker's or friend's spouse. And we especially cannot compare our spouses to those that we see on the television or big screen. The grass usually isn't greener on the other side. Maybe it starts off green but eventually, due to neglect and a lack of time to always weed it and feed it, it has a tendency to start dying. We probably have greener grass right in our own back yard.

As in every other aspect of life, "It's all in how you look at it."

After graduating, as I have already related, I made that leap to a different, smaller bank, which later would only prove to have its own set of internal challenges. However, my experience there was a good one, because it allowed me to realize some strengths and talents that I actually had forgotten I was blessed to possess.

After participating in their training program for those desiring to become managers, I had the opportunity to make a few presentations. During these times, I remembered how much I had enjoyed public speaking, and silently wished that I could somehow incorporate that back into my life. The speaking experiences that came, re-ignited my desire to motivate and uplift others on a grand scale. For many years, I had been searching to find out what my purpose was in life. I knew that I had now found that purpose, but at the moment I was unsure how to fulfill it. Meanwhile, there was my discomfort with the atmosphere at this new bank, and the attitude of my manager.

So I did what I always do when faced with a challenge that I don't know the solution to: Pray.

But the answers that I would receive were not what I had expected. Each time that I prayed, the answer was always very boldly placed in my face. In spite of the boldness of the answers, I found it very hard to conceive that I was being told to make a huge move that would definitely test my faith.

This point in my business career was extremely taxing because at every turn, new problems were coming up at this new company, and I felt I was being deliberately misled. When I had initially interviewed, they told me that I could make the six figures that I was earning at my prior company. Well, after being employed as a staff appraiser at the new company for nearly a year, I was earning about 55-60% less than at my prior company.

At first I decided to live with that on the premise that I would definitely earn significantly more when promoted to manager. But after successfully holding two managerial positions, I was still earning about 50% less than at my parent company, and it was nowhere near six figures.

My husband and I resolved that I would not allow money to be the reason for my departure from this job. The new company had recently merged with a larger bank that I had actually wanted to work for prior to coming here, but they did not have offices on the West Coast. In spite of the financial letdown, there were still new opportunities resulting from the merger. Because I was not too fond of the smaller company's culture and a few of their methods of operation, I found the merger to be a blessing, and a reason to stick around a little while longer.

Upon accepting my second managerial position, which was as a district appraisal leader for the West Los Angeles Appraisal office for the company, I had been led to believe that I would have close to a full staff. Unfortunately, my first day on the job, I was presented with less than half the staff I'd been promised, plus heavy volume, and only a tiny increase in my salary. Add to this a regional manager who wanted to micro-manage me, and a 1.5-hour (one-way, that is) commute in bumper-to-bumper traffic. The handwriting was on the wall.

My husband had been suggesting to me that I quit for almost a year prior. However, if I did that, we would have to utilize a portion of our savings and some of my retirement.

During this period of career stress, the family stresses also peaked. Due to a rough period that my mom, Daniel and I had experienced with my niece Karla, my husband and I decided (as her legal guardians) that it would be best if Karla went to live permanently with her godmother.

Daniel and I had asked Karla what would make her happy and assist her both academically and emotionally, and she indicated that she wanted to live with her godmother. Since Karla had spent more time with her godmother than she did with my mother or me when Peggy was alive, this would be a pretty decent alternative for my niece. Daniel and I both felt that this would give her a desire to live her life in a respectful manner, since the respect that she had demonstrated towards my mother was next to nil. More than likely, this disrespect was a direct result of how Peggy had treated my mother in the presence of her children. Karla had learned this behavior from her mother.

But this was a difficult decision for me. As it turned out, Karla had been secretly in communication with her godmother, despite our family's forbidding her to do so. Upon learning of the nature of her conversations and visits with her godmother, my husband and I knew that things needed to change for Karla.

The year prior, we had moved Sammuelle and Karla into our home and put them in the schools near us because their grades had suffered while they lived with my mother. Daniel and I felt that having them at our home would allow us to help them with their homework and provide some much-needed academic tutoring.

Over the course of that school year, Sammuelle and Karla received private tutoring in reading and reading comprehension from a center in Palos Verdes, which I had found through the school district. As a result of the No Child Left Behind Act, several local tutoring centers were providing select services for students in LAUSD. After the initial sessions were completed, Sammuelle demonstrated some improvement, but Karla showed very little. Determined to see her improve, I subsequently enrolled her in a different tutoring center in hopes of increasing her math skills. Upon completion of this program, also bi-weekly, Karla finally demonstrated improvement.

By the end of the school year, Karla successfully culminated from middle school, and Sammuelle was promoted to the 12th grade. They returned to their home with my mother, and I enrolled the two of them at the local high school. Later we found out that Karla was exhibiting promiscuous behavior with boys who were likely affiliated with a gang. While living with my mother, Karla had apparently skipped school and was inviting boys to her house during school hours, while her grandmother was at work and her brother Sammuelle was at school.

One morning I had stopped by Mom's house to drop off lunch money for Sammuelle. After entering the house, I heard the shower running in Sammuelle's bathroom. Instantly I felt upset since I was utilizing my work time in order to leave him lunch money. I stood in the hallway and waited so that I could surprise my nephew when he came out of the bathroom. When the shower turned off and the bathroom door opened, to my dismay, it was Karla. Here it was 10:00

in the morning when she should have been in school, and she was just now taking a shower?

Karla was very surprised to find me standing there -- she was coming into the hallway to put the cordless telephone receiver back on the base. In my naiveté it didn't occur to me that she might have been expecting company. This was the furthest thing from my mind, since I would not have even dared such truancy when I was 14.

"Why are you still at home?" I demanded to know.

"I woke up late," she said.

To which I responded, "Two hours late!"

Disgusted and disappointed, I made Karla get dressed, and took her to school. Then I phoned Daniel to tell him what happened. We agreed to meet at Mom's home that evening after he got off from work.

When evening came, my daughter and I made it to Mom's address a few minutes early, so we sat in the car in front of the house and waited for Daniel. While waiting, I suddenly noticed a young African-American male emerge from the neighbor's driveway to the west of our house. This was disturbing, since our neighbors on that side were Hispanic and never have African-American visitors, other than my husband, my daughter or myself.

So I called Daniel and told him what I had just seen. Before I could even finish describing the guy, another young African-American male emerged from the driveway. At this point, Daniel was only a few blocks away and managed to see the guys walking once he had entered the neighborhood. He followed them to see if they lived nearby; however, after several moments, he realized they were not from our immediate community. So he turned around and came to meet us.

When Daniel arrived, he went to the side of the house that the young men had emerged from, which happened to be where Karla's room is located. He then came back and told me, "Go look at your niece's window."

As I approached the window, Karla's blinds were open and bent, the light was on, and she was standing in her room with her pajamas on, which happened to be a ribbed cotton tank top and regular fleece pajama bottoms. Since she was dressed for bed, she was not wearing a bra, and the cleavage of her size 36D breasts was well exposed. It was October and almost 7 p.m., so it was quite dark outside, and the man in the moon was witnessing this entire event. From the looks of her blinds and bent window screen, it appeared that the two guys had been putting their hands through the window to fondle her.

This was a devastating realization. Never in a million years did I think I would be experiencing something like this with my 14-year old niece.

After entering the house, and explaining to my mother what we had just witnessed, and the earlier incident, we had Karla come into the dining room so that the three of us could speak with her. We found out that one of the guys, the eldest, was supposedly her boyfriend. This young man had apparently dropped out of school and was approximately 17 years of age. Karla only knew him by his nickname, or "gang" name.

"What's his legal name?" we asked.

"I don't know," she shrugged.

We also learned that Karla had been stealing money from my mother, and giving it to her so-called boyfriend. Finally, as we found out more about Karla's sexual activity, she revealed some very disturbing things that brought me to tears.

So I told my mother, "It's probably best if Karla goes to live with Charles and Tanya. We need to remove her from this environment so that neither you nor she will be in any danger, considering that the young gentlemen we saw are known gang members."

Right away, I called my brother Charles and asked him to come by and pick up Karla. When Charles arrived, he shared with Karla the same concerns that the rest of us were feeling, that she could get AIDS from participating in such behaviors.

"Do you realize," I asked her, "that AIDS is the same disease that took your mother's life? Don't you realize the consequences of your behavior?"

So Karla was relocated with Charles and Tanya. I completed the necessary school papers for her enrollment, authorizing the two of them to act as her caretakers during this period. After Karla had lived with Charles and Tanya for several months, and appeared to have become acclimated to her new school and environment, Daniel felt strongly that I should attempt to get her some counseling or therapy. Her behavior could possibly be a form of acting out because of her mother's death, and the loss and void that she had had to endure, especially considering the closeness that she and her mother shared.

After lengthy research, and numerous phone calls to various practitioners and therapists approved by our HMO and within our medical network, I was finally able to secure a therapist. Every other Saturday, I would pick Karla up and bring her to see her therapist, who was located in Torrance. On certain Fridays, depending on Charles' schedule, he would drop Karla off at my mother's, so that I could take her to her therapy appointments on Saturday. Towards the end of the traditional school year, during the summer, Karla revealed some things to her therapist that were shared with me during one of her sessions, which required that I remove Karla from Charles and Tanya's home.

Chapter 24

From Family Pain to Great Endeavors

It was also during this trying time that Karla revealed her desire to see her father and his side of her family. Karla indicated how much she missed her father and her half sister. Up to this period, it was always a given that she could never be alone with her father after he had kissed her in the lips despite the fact that he had full-blown AIDS. Additionally, because of her father's abusive and ignorant behaviors, he was not allowed at our home, only the home of Charles and Tanya. These were the rules, for her protection, and the therapist agreed. The therapist shared with Karla that this was probably for her own benefit. This would conclude Karla's therapy.

Over the next month, Karla continued to voice her deep desires to be allowed to visit with the paternal side of her family. Her half-sister was approximately 17 years of age, and lived in L.A. with her maternal grandmother. After I spent much alone time with Karla, she revealed that my mother had repeatedly said that she would not allow Karla to see her father, or spend any long visitation period with her half-sister.

By this point, my nephew Sammuelle had finally passed the California High School Exit Exam and met all requirements to graduate. After his graduation ceremony, my mother had a barbecue at our house to celebrate the occasion. My sister Margaret and her family had come down, and my sister Tanya and her family were in attendance as well. At one point during the afternoon, Margaret decided to go to the local market and asked Karla to come along with her. Upon their return, Karla was in tears.

When asked what had happened, Margaret shrugged. "All of a sudden Karla just started crying for no apparent reason," she said. That day Karla never revealed why she was apparently so upset.

During a subsequent visit with Karla, Daniel and I tried to find out more about her feelings and the many events that had taken place in her life over the last year. It was during this time that I asked her what would make her the happiest, to which she replied, "To live with my godmother." She also felt that this would allow her to visit with her father and his relatives, which also included her oldest sister.

So I asked Karla, "Would that help you to strive to do your best and feel good about who you are?"

Her face brightened up happily. "Yes, it would," she said.

Daniel and I looked at each other, feeling that this was probably going to be our best hope for Karla.

Often, when I was able to spend time alone with Karla, she would disclose to me some situations and events about her life that I truly would have rather have not known, especially those about her very active sex life. When she shared one particular incident with me, I asked her, "How did that make you feel? Did it make you feel good on the inside?"

"Now I know it wasn't good for me," she admitted. "But at the time I really didn't give it much thought."

One afternoon, Karla revealed another significant point. She had just had her annual physical exam with the pediatrician, and we were now on our way to Walgreen's to have her birth control prescription filled—something that I never thought I would need to do for my 14-year old niece. In the conversation, Karla shared with me once again how much she missed her father.

"I really want to be able to see him," she said. "At my mom's funeral, I didn't like it when Charles got into an argument with my dad and said that he wanted to hurt him. It made me mad. My dad is still my dad."

At this point, I realized that the longer Karla was prevented from seeing her father, the more she would continue to misbehave. As her aunt and legal guardian, it was my responsibility to do not only what was physically best for Karla, but also what was mentally best for her as well. For as long as I can remember, ever since my sister died, Karla would remain quiet during family events. But after we finally allowed her to visit her father, his family and her sister, she opened up and almost became like a different person, and not necessarily in a bad way. I realized that by allowing Karla to be amongst her paternal family, she was able to find out who she was and why.

One day after Karla had spent a few visits with her paternal family, she shared with me the many things that she learned about her father and his behavior, and also the many things that she had in common with him and her sister. I must admit, some of the things I would have rather not heard. But again, this is who she is. None of us gets to choose who our parents are and Karla is no exception. Should I fault her for who she is? By all means no!

Having all these experiences with Karla actually taught me a valuable lesson, and also gave me some enlightenment about my own situation with my biological father. My mother had decided, for her own reasons, that I would never know who my real father was, and if it weren't for the pressure from my aunts, she would have taken that secret to her grave. Would this have been fair to me? To my father and paternal brothers? Absolutely not! Sometimes you must learn when to let go and let God work it all out. As humans, and -- I'm sorry to say but especially -- as Christians, we have the tendency to take God's place by acting in our own accord and not necessarily for the good of others.

Again, everything happens for a reason, and it happens when it is supposed to. But as humans we must learn that we don't know everything, nor do we have all of the answers. Sometimes we parents will attempt to protect our children from certain harm, only to find that we actually wind up placing them smack in the middle of that exact harm. I've truly learned to put things in God's hands because He knows and sees all things. So, if God truly knows and sees all, who am I to judge what is best for someone else when I only know what I can see with my own two eyes, and can hear with my own two ears, which is only from one perspective—mine! I might also mention that most of the time when we get wind of something from someone, we're only getting one side of the story. There are always at least two sides to every story, especially if there are two people involved. The more people that get added to the equation, the more sides to the story you will have.

This is exactly what I shared with my mother about Karla going to live with her godmother, that I had prayed about it and put it in God's hands.

"If we truly believe in God and know of His power, we must therefore trust that things will work out for the best," I told Mom.

My mother responded dryly, "The devil also has power."

My heart sank when I heard this from her. It told me that I was not going to be able to share with her the least bit of light that I had gotten on this situation. That kind of dialogue was what I continued to hear from both my mother and my oldest sister Margaret.

One day my sister Margaret even went so far as to tell me, "It's your husband who is causing you to feel that way about Karla going to live with her godmother."

On top of the stress that I was experiencing at work, this comment was just the beginning of major stress that I began to feel from my family over Karla's future. Margaret and my mother took it upon themselves to involve not just my immediate family, which would include my mother and my siblings, but also my aunts and cousins. Before I knew it, the whole maternal side of the family was on an anti-Veronica campaign. The word out was that my husband had caused me to change. In addition to this, as we would learn from both Sammuelle and Karla, certain members of the family were commenting about how Daniel and I thought we were white, and that Karla was not going to live with her godmother because her godmother was not blood and therefore was not a part of the family.

Another part of this campaign revolved around Sammuelle. Prior to his graduating, he would be taught how to drive by non other than his non-blood uncle, my husband Daniel. We still had Daniel's 1990 Honda Civic with a manual transmission, so on many weekends and afternoons, Daniel would take Sammuelle out to practice driving it.

Daniel and I had agreed that Sammuelle could purchase the Civic from us for $150, though at the time it was probably worth a minimum of $500. Daniel knew that I strongly believe in working for what you want, and neither he nor I was ever given anything. Everything we had managed to accomplish and acquire, we worked for. We definitely had assistance and mentors along the way, but we still had to put in the work. I was not going to have it any other way with our daughter, nor the niece and nephew who were our responsibility. As working parents, I did not want any of them getting the impression that anything in life was free or effortlessly gained. All things worthy will involve some form of work whether mental or physical, and sometimes both.

As a part of our agreement with Sammuelle, he would also have a job so that he could afford to purchase the car and have it re-registered under his name. Despite this initial agreement, Daniel decided that we should go ahead and let Sammuelle have the car so that he could fill out job applications or drive to the few other places where he needed to go. Daniel's decision was based on Sammuelle being a good kid. However, I was concerned. The car was still registered in Daniel's name so if Sammuelle became involved in an accident, we would be liable.

After a few months had passed and Sammuelle hadn't found a job, I told Daniel that we should take the car back until Sammuelle had secured some form of employment. Hesitantly following my request, Daniel sent Sammuelle a text message asking if he could bring the car back. Because he's a good kid, Sammuelle brought the car back to our house the very next morning.

Upon learning this and knowing that Sammuelle would spend most of his days and late nights filling out job applications at the local Internet café, my sister Margaret decided to call me and let me know just how she felt about us taking the car back.

"I know it was Daniel who made Sammuelle give the car back," she stormed at me. "And anything could happen to Sammuelle while he's walking home from the Internet Café at one o'clock in the morning!"

Unfortunately her phone call came on a Saturday morning when I was already stressed and depressed about my job. After hanging up the phone, I was sitting on Daniel's lap, and just burst into tears. At that moment, I decided that I couldn't take anymore.

Late that evening, Daniel and I had a long conversation that would last into the wee hours of the morning. It was then that I decided that Karla could not go to live with her godmother, mainly due to the stress and trauma I was getting from my family. It was true that Karla would do well with her godmother, who had already made plans to enroll her in a high school where there were administrators on board to see to it that Karla would not get into any trouble. In addition, Karla's godmother had made plans to have Karla participate in a local children's ministry, which was actually administered by one of our church members. After several conversations with Karla's godmother, I had honestly felt that this was going to work out quite well for Karla -- only to have that dream attacked by people who call themselves Christian but say, do and act otherwise.

A few nights later I went over to my mother's to break the news to Karla. But her godmother had already given her the news. My niece was crying uncontrollably.

"Why can't I go live with my godmother?" she asked me.

"Because I can't take on the whole family," I answered her honestly. "They are all against the decision, and I'm under a lot of stress about it. I'm so sorry. But maybe it will work out okay for you in Mississippi."

My mother was relocating to Mississippi and was hoping to take Karla with her. She was sure that a different environment on the other side of the country would probably do Karla some good.

"Getting her out of this crazy L.A. life would be the best for her," Mom said.

I knew that in many cases this holds true, and could only hope that the same would happen with Karla.

Before leaving for Mississippi, Karla asked if she could spend some days with her godmother. Despite my mother's rejections, I told her that this would be fine, as it was the least that I could do after nearly breaking her heart. After a while Karla told me that she had gotten used to the idea of living in Mississippi and thought it will be ok for her. I responded by telling her that it will be whatever she makes of it.

"If you see it in a positive way," I said, " then that will be what you get."

In November, Karla and my mother successfully relocated to Mississippi. It had been previously agreed upon that Karla would spend Christmas with her paternal family. One of her paternal aunts had already secured an airline ticket for her. However, when it came time for Christmas break, my mother would not allow Karla to go and visit her father, his family and her godmother.

"It wouldn't be good for Karla because of the way those people are," Mama insisted.

In a nutshell, all the familial events around Karla would be partially responsible for my new lengthy bouts with depression. This tension and anxiety, coupled with that which I was already experiencing with work, sent me to places inside myself where I had never gone before, although I didn't realize it at the time. It wasn't until many months later, after speaking with a close friend of mine who is a pediatrician, that I would realize the culprits initially responsible for my depression. She informed me that the high stress that I was under sometimes causes the body's hormones to be thrown off, which will cause depression and/or sometimes create the onset of menopause.

Meanwhile in September, prior to my mother's and Karla's move, I gave notice to my divisional manager that I was resigning. This was actually the second time that I had initiated my resignation. I had previously given notice in July, right after being assigned the district appraisal leader position and finding that I had been lied to again. This did not sit well with the national manager. She informed me that she saw me as a valuable asset to the company -- to have me walk away would be a great loss. Therefore, she would make arrangements in my favor in order to keep me on board.

"Think about your decision," she said, "and let me know where you want to go from that position." She knew that I truly did not want to remain a district appraisal leader.

After deliberating, I decided that I didn't want to leave them high and dry. So I told her, "I will stay on board long enough for you to find a replacement for me."

But August came and went, and it didn't appear that they were searching for my replacement. I continued to think about the alternatives that the national manager had given me. I could either become the district appraisal leader of the Torrance Appraisal Office, which was located only about 10 minutes from my home. Or, I could leave management altogether and revert back to a staff appraiser position in the Torrance office, with close to the six-figure salary that I was previously earning at my parent company. The one drawback to going back was that I would be under the leadership of the district and regional managers who had given me so much grief previously.

I believe this was God's way of ensuring that I followed the path that He had already prepared for me. He knew that, once I remembered these facts, I wouldn't even dream of returning to that office as a staff appraiser. It was time for me to depart. September would be my last month as an employee. I re-submitted my letter of resignation, with no intentions of being swayed in any other direction.

Lesson XVIII: *Faith is knowing that the things, which you cannot see, truly can and will exist.*

By October 1st, I was stepping out on faith that all would be well. Semi-retired from my job, with two mortgages, I knew that this was nothing but faith! I had already told myself that I could not write about something that I didn't strongly believe to be true myself. This was definitely my chance to live by my own words and beliefs. It was now or never. I was now given the blessing and opportunity to pursue the finishing of my book, and to spend some much needed time with my family, especially my daughter. These were my two main goals at the moment.

This was going to be my daughter's first year of middle school, which is a very important time in any child's life. Because of my staff appraiser position at my parent company, I had grown accustomed to always being able to work my schedule around her schedule. It wasn't until I had left my parent company and began my new journey with the smaller company, that I would meet with challenges in working my schedule around her schedule. As I had stated previously, the handwriting was on the wall, and in my newly appointed management position, it turned out that I had even less flexibility in my schedule.

As a result of faith, my husband and I were able to sell our primary residence for a sizable profit during a depressed market, in just over 3 months. Even after deducting the costs of our expenses for improvements and other miscellaneous costs utilized for the property, we still realized a significant profit. It was our initial intention to downsize our lifestyle in order that I could confidently enjoy taking a hiatus to spend time with our daughter and finishing this book.

When we banked our net profit, Daniel quickly reminded me, "You know – we just earned your prior salary from your parent company!"

Better yet, God had already prepared us for being able to live off of only 55% of it, which was my most recent salary for the prior 1.5 years.

After we sold our home, we moved back into our first home. This property was located in the South Bay, only slightly closer to Daniel's place of employment. Our net gains would allow us to donate a portion to charitable causes, pay off our credit-card debt, purchase a desperately needed new car for Daniel, make nice improvements to the home, and still have residuals to both save and invest.

As Robert T. Kiyosaki indicates in his book, *Rich Dad Poor Dad*, this is one of the best methods of accumulating wealth. Allow your assets to pay for those luxury items that you desire, instead of going into debt in order to finance your lifestyle of luxury. Financing luxury is something that I have honestly never believed in. True wealth is when you're able to utilize your discretionary income for luxuries, and not have concern as to whether you can "truly" afford it.

The real-estate profit earned was in excess of the retirement income that I was also able to enjoy and utilize. Because of the years that I had spent and income earned at my parent company, coupled with my frugality, I was able to amass a substantial retirement and savings fund that would allow me to enjoy my current hiatus. Throughout this entire experience, I held onto the mindset that living is giving. There is no doubt in my mind that this played a great part in the wealth that we have been blessed to amass.

Chapter 25

For Closure and Inspiration.... Be Inspired

Final Lesson: *As you share your talents with the world, the world will share its talents with you.*

Now that I can look back and view parts of the journey that have already occurred, I am able to see even more blessings than I ever saw before, and to know that I am undoubtedly on the right path.

God doesn't lead us astray. If we look to Him for answers, He will provide them. I cannot even begin to express my joy that I was financially able to quit my job in order to not only pursue my passion, but also do what makes me the happiest...and that is being there for my daughter. As long as I know that she is well and taken care of, my days get all the more easier and brighter. In addition, to spend more quality time with my family is priceless.

There have been and will continue to be struggles, challenges and misfortune. However, I know that each of them is only temporary, and when they're done, victory is on the horizon. Make no mistake about it. In life, balance must always exist. Fortune has to prevail in order for misfortune to get invited. Trials have to occur so that triumphs could be born as well. Life is a balance. We must only remember to see it in this way.

For those of you experiencing difficult times in your life, I would strongly encourage you to seek your source for guidance and strength. When my sister was dying and I was parrying with my husband about her two children, I prayed. When my sister had given up on life and thrown in the towel, I prayed. Tell me a time that you know of when I appeared chaotic, depressed or lost, and I will tell you that it was a time when I wasn't turning to God, my true source for direction and strength to make it through.

After you read my story, it is my hope that you realize there's a positive aspect in every negative situation. Think about the complete situation first, and study how it has impacted your life in a positive manner. Did it make you stronger? Are you now closer to someone than you were before the incident happened? Do you now have a new way of completing a task or handling a situation? There are many ways to look at any situation. As Dr. Wayne Dyer says, "When you change the way you look at things, the things you look at change."

So change your outlook on life and on the various circumstances of your life. See the lesson in every situation where you may not have come out the winner, or where you may have been hurt. If you see the lesson, you will learn and grow. See only the result and you only continue to experience the trauma. Move past the pain and embrace the challenge. Challenges will make you stronger as long as you continue to see them this way.

Whether we admit it or not, we have all endured some form of emotional pain, and through its course we have possibly questioned God and the reasons we had to experience such trauma in our lives. Speaking only from experience, I can honestly say that these unfortunate and probably untimely circumstances presented themselves in order to prompt some form of spiritual growth in my life. Whether I wanted to acknowledge them as such through their relentless existence is moot. We all must recognize that struggles and unfortunate events must explode into our lives in order for us to experience triumph and perseverance. As I mentioned previously, this creates the balance that is the prevailing force of life.

However, this is the selfish reason for pain's existence. The unselfish reason that we have such experiences is to circumvent the possibility of this ever occurring in someone else's life. God obviously felt that we were strong enough to handle such agony; otherwise another perfect soul would have been selected. As best that we know how, we must learn to temporarily embrace those tormenting challenges that we endure. Embrace them, knowing that they too will pass and later become a story in which you can share about your victory over each of them.

I must admit to each of you that in describing my story as "From Welfare to Wealth," I know that this has been true for all of my life. Even though I was a child on welfare, I never considered my family or myself as being poor or in need. As long as we had food to eat, a place to call home and clothing to cover our bodies, there was nothing else to actually "need."

As I came to writing the end of this book, I realized even more that life truly is how you see it and what you make of it. We may have been on welfare, and probably had less than lots of other families, but this is not how I chose to look at my life. As long as I had God by my side and the aforementioned bare necessities, with the ability to think for myself, I was able to maintain a wealth mentality. The way I look at it, television is not required for survival. If it were, there would be millions of deaths across the globe because not everyone owns a television. Candy, a nicer car or home, fancy clothes and jewelry are not necessities for one's survival.

Your life is how you perceive it to be. No one else can form this vision for you, although some may try. Always see your life from the positive aspects. If you want your life to be more fulfilling in any way, visualize your life the way you want it to be. As I've stated previously, whatever is meant for you is what you will get -- because no one else besides you has the ability to take it away or prevent you from receiving it. Associate yourself with positive people, and as the saying goes, "Never let anyone steal your sunshine, even on a rainy day."

You have the power to become great, but you must first find your purpose and live it out to your fullest potential. Live your life so that you are always a blessing to someone else. We are not put on this earth to accumulate wealth, only to distribute the wealth that we have been blessed to obtain. We are all wealthy as long as we see ourselves this way. Distributing the wealth that you have been blessed to receive doesn't have to be monetary wealth. It could of course be mental wealth, spiritual wealth, a wealth of knowledge, physical ability, etc. Give of that which God has given to you. The more you give, the more you will have to give, for this is a Universal Law. Know that you are great, and expect nothing less. As you think, so shall you be. Think greatness, and this is what you shall become.

As I said at the beginning of this book, we all have a story. I have told you my story. What is yours? It's important for more stories to be told – the stories about people learning from their lives. And if you don't feel the desire to write your own story, tell someone so that they may write it.

I'm a firm believer that if every person on the Earth wrote their story, there would be no need for television because we all would be connected through books -- through words that will touch our spirits in ways that no Oscar-nominated movie can ever get to do. (Although if you think about it, many if not most of the Oscar-nominated movies, and even the non-Oscar nominated movies that have really touched your life, were probably based on true stories. I know that the movies that have truly touched my own life were mostly based on true stories.)

We are all stories waiting to be told, so that our sisters and brothers of all colors, shapes and sizes throughout the World will know who we are without ever having met us personally. This is how we are connected—through our human spirits, our lives that someone else is dying to know about. If this book has touched you in any way, it is your obligation — your direction from God -- to share your own story with the world. As human beings, we need one another's stories because they keep us living and help us refrain from making mistakes that have already been made for us.

So let us hear your story -- it will be like food to our souls. Please don't let us starve.

Author Insights

On Buying and Maintaining Real Estate

When preparing to buy a home, do not start by consulting with a realtor or by going out to look at houses. Do not do this! These are not the first steps to take when contemplating buying a piece of real estate. First and foremost, you need to know how much house you can afford. Therefore, I would strongly encourage you to first, (even before going out to get pre-qualified for a mortgage), look at your current financial situation and determine how much _you_ can honestly and truly afford to pay each month towards your mortgage, and please be honest with yourself. This is what I did each time that we prepared to purchase a new property.

First I would look at our expenses to determine how much we were spending each month, and how much we could spend on a monthly house payment. When looking at our expenses, I included such things as our daughter's private school tuition (during those times that she attended private school) because this is one of those items that are _not_ included by the lender when determining your eligibility/pre-qualification for a mortgage. I would consider private school expenses as *hidden* expenses because for the most part they are excluded from a family's monthly expenses when the analysis is being done to qualify them for a home mortgage. If you are planning for your child to continue to attend private school, then you must include these expenses in your total monthly expenditures.

Once you have determined how much you feel you can afford to pay each month for a mortgage, the second step is to consult with a lender to get pre-qualified. Once the lender has pre-qualified you and you are comfortable with the monthly mortgage payment (including the taxes and insurance), you will now know how much house you can truly afford.

Caution: Do not allow a lender or mortgage broker to convince you that you can afford more home by utilizing creative financial products such as interest only loans, hybrid mortgages or adjustable rate mortgages (ARM's). These mortgage products have largely contributed to the recent mortgage melt down. Millions of people purchased homes that they truly could not afford because they utilized the aforementioned loan products.

If you are considering purchasing a home that needs work, you must also include in your budget/monthly finances, the amount of money it will take to improve/repair the property. Do not assume that you will be able to handle it once you have purchased the property. If the property needs work, consult with a contractor or home improvement professional to find out approximately how much it will take to at least make the property livable to your standards. The worst thing that you can do is get excited about the house, fall in love with it, purchase it, and later find out once you've started making mortgage payments, that you won't be able to fix it up the way you want. Make sure you are well aware of the costs involved for repairs so that you can make the necessary financial preparations to complete the repairs.

Once you know how much house you can afford, you are now able to consult with a Realtor to show you homes within your price range. Experienced Realtors that have been in the real estate business for at least 7 years or more (preferably 10 years), will know the areas that they serve and will therefore know which areas are within your price range. Realtors with this much experience are able to assist with the millions of questions that you are undoubtedly going to have about the entire buying process.

After you have purchased your home, you might begin to receive letters in the mail from various lenders regarding refinancing your mortgage. ***When should you refinance a mortgage?*** Refinancing a mortgage should be considered for a few logical reasons. If you currently have a 15 or 30 year fixed rate on your mortgage and it is at least .5% or more, higher than the current interest rates being offered, then you might want to consider refinancing your mortgage. However, even when this condition exists, if you are planning to sell your home within the next 5 years, it may not be a good idea to refinance. You must first do a little homework to find out how much money you would save over those 5 years by refinancing. If the amount that you will save is less than or equal to the amount of money that it will cost you to refinance, then it is probably not a good idea to refinance. On the other hand, if by refinancing your mortgage, you will save $5,000 or more (after the costs of refinancing have been allowed for) over the 5 years, refinancing might be a good option for you.

Another reason that you might consider refinancing your mortgage would be to purchase a second home or investment property. When you refinance a mortgage, depending on the amount of equity that you have in your home, you may be able to get cash out for the purchase of the additional property. Utilizing your existing home to purchase additional properties is a good way to build real estate investments. However, unless you're able to pay cash for the additional property, this should only be done if you are financially able to afford the mortgage payment on the additional property. I strongly encourage you to do a little investigating to find out how much cash you can get out of your home, and utilize this as a gauge as to how much you can afford for the additional property.

If the property you are going to purchase is an investment property and you are unable to buy it outright by paying cash, the safest way to ensure that you are always able to pay the mortgage is to only buy an investment property in which you can afford the mortgage in addition to your current mortgage and expenses. This is why I emphasize doing some investigating to find out how much cash you're able to take out of your home, and use this to determine how much of an investment property you can afford. Once you know how much cash you can take out, I would then follow the steps above to purchase your second home or investment property. Also, when buying an investment property, one of the golden rules is to only purchase investment properties that you wouldn't mind living in yourself. If the property is in a community in which you wouldn't want to live in, then I suggest that you not purchase that property. The reason for this is because there may come a day when you might have to live in that property. So if that day does come, you will feel comfortable both financially and mentally.

Other reasons that you might decide to refinance your mortgage would be to purchase a new car, or make home improvements. Again, you could get cash out in order to buy the car outright and not have to finance the vehicle. Do some research first because recently, many of the car companies have offered financing rates that are well below mortgage rates, so make sure that you find out how much it would be to finance a car through the dealerships finance department. In some cases, the manufacturers have offered 0% financing, and I don't think you can beat that!

When considering refinancing in order to complete home improvements, you should first explore the improvements that you would like to do and the costs involved. Once you know the costs, you can then determine which improvements you are able to actually do once you find out how much cash you are able to get out. But in either case, whether you are considering a car purchase or home improvements, only refinance if you are comfortable with your new mortgage payment.

If you follow this simple advice when it comes to real estate, you can be on your way to establishing wealth through real estate. As with any investment however, you must use serious caution and know what you're getting into by first doing your research, and following the steps outlined above. Real estate is a great way to build wealth, but you must utilize discretion and consult with the appropriate professionals to ensure that you are making a good decision. Also, one of the rules that I have always believed in that will help you to buy at the right time is to purchase real estate after a boom when the market has taken a dive. Do not purchase real estate when there is a buying frenzy and everywhere you turn you hear about buying real estate. You'll hear expressions such as, "If you don't buy now, you'll never be able to purchase real estate." Whenever the market is hot and buyers are fighting over properties, this is usually not a good time to purchase real estate.

If you utilize patience, the perfect time will come to buy real estate. We are in that time right now. The boom is over, and there are plenty of distressed properties out there to choose from. You always want to buy real estate during a depressed market or when the market is on its way to recovery. This is when you will get the best deals and prices. If you buy real estate during a boom, you may not be able to build equity as fast as you would if you had bought during a depressed or recovery period. Keep this in mind and abide by this rule, and you will do quite well with your real estate investments. People who listened when I counseled them about when to buy real estate have done quite well for themselves. Real estate has been my livelihood for the past 17 years, and I have learned a great deal over this time period. The knowledge that I gained has allowed my husband and I to do very well financially, so I am passing the information on so that you too can do the same. Again, if you follow these steps and rules, you will get quite far in the real estate game. I wish you the best of luck in your endeavors.

On Depression

In my bout with depression I would not have known how other people experience such a powerful state of sadness had I not gone through the same thing. Depression is nothing to be mocked. To anyone who is currently depressed, my heart goes out to you. If you are experiencing depression in your life right now, I feel that it is my obligation to share with you how I was able to deal with this painful mental state. If you've made it successfully through depression, you have reason to celebrate life with new meaning, because I know firsthand the devastation that is felt while being under this dark cloud.

Merriam Webster's definition of depression is as follows: "a psychoneurotic or psychotic disorder marked especially by sadness, inactivity, difficulty in thinking and concentration, a significant increase or decrease in appetite and time spent sleeping, feelings of dejection and hopelessness, and sometimes suicidal tendencies." To this definition I might also add, "lack of motivation, and difficulty in completing daily activities." For the most part, these were my symptoms during my depression episodes. It was important that I add the latter portion because this was the part of depression that seemed to visit me on a daily basis, blatantly causing me to acknowledge that I was depressed.

My depression actually felt like a form of paralysis. For me, there is no other way to describe it. When I was depressed, I couldn't bring myself to get out of bed in the morning. Or shall I say I had no *desire* whatsoever to get out of bed. As a matter of fact, during my periods of depression, each night before I went to bed, I would hope and pray that something major would happen and the morning would never come. This is depression in the worst sense. Describing it as a paralysis is the best way to put a face on it due to the manner in which it zaps every ounce of energy, ambition, desire and willpower that you ever had. At least this is what it feels like, especially to someone who had never experienced such negative desires, thoughts and behaviors, despite whatever horrible circumstances may have been present.

When I was 11, depression didn't sink in when my dad died, although he was an extraordinarily strong force in my life. When I was 18, depression never came about when I found out that my dad wasn't whom I thought he was; nor did it show its ugly face when I wrecked the truck that I had bought just before I was to leave for college. And the list goes on, as you very well know at this point.

Now, after months of being semi-retired and attempting to start my new businesses does the depression re-emerge and put never-ending stops to my efforts. I continuously asked myself several times over, "Why am I going through this?" On days that I was experiencing depression, I would only answer my cell phone if it were my husband or my daughter, and occasionally my mother, depending on my mood. There would be days in which I couldn't even bring myself to shower until about 12 o'clock noon at the earliest. This was completely the opposite of who I was and wanted to be. Being like this only hurt me even more because when you're going through it you feel as though your life is going to end in ruin. And this is the way that I felt 3 weeks out of each month.

There was absolutely no way that I was going to get my businesses going while I was in such poor shape. Sometimes people would call to inquire about possibly having an appraisal, or about a possible consulting opportunity, only to have their phone call go unreturned for approximately two weeks.

Up to this point in my life, I felt that I had lived a fairly decent life, living by the Golden Rule, treating others as I desired to be treated. In addition, I knew that I was always helping others along my life's journey because you just never know what tomorrow may bring. Many nights and days I would meditate at home, or go sit at the beach and wonder why I was experiencing such a horrid mental time that I seemingly had no control over. Never in my earlier life had I experienced such feelings, despite the fact that I had gone through some pretty devastating times.

During the episodes, it felt as though there was an impeding force over me that could not be broken. Each morning that depression showed its horrific face, I would just lie in bed wishing for time to stand still so that I could get myself together. I would apply the same logic every night that I went to bed depressed. It was always my hope that the night could go on forever so that I wasn't required to make any decisions the next day, even if the decision was as simple as picking out an outfit to wear.

These episodes would last between four to seven days. Then, miraculously, after I spent time exercising, they would disappear for a few days. Without fail, however, the depression always returned. Day after day this scenario would get repeated while I constantly asked God, "Why me?"

Prior to this period of being depressed, I always seemed to have an abundance of energy. Regardless of how much I had to get done, relative to my work and my home life, I would get all tasks completed without a second thought. I was never one to complain about my situation or circumstances. Throughout my lifetime, I had learned to just deal with whatever life threw my way. Complaining about it just wasn't my cup of tea because it didn't seem to do anybody any good.

But suddenly there I was -- depressed and wondering how the heck did I get that way?

Finally the day arrived when I was fed up. I was sick and tired of being sick and tired.

Desperate to do something, anything, I started physically taking punches at the air as if I was actually fighting someone, which in my mind was depression. The next day I began telling myself that I was happy and successful, and did this every time that those unhappy moods were trying to seep back into my system. The second thing that I did was changing my environment. I was tired of looking at the same walls of my home, day in and day out, so fortunately the holidays had arrived and I booked a trip to go visit my brother and his family in Maryland.

All these desperate measures helped...but only a little. I finally realized that I had to seek professional help. So I discussed my condition with Daniel just to make sure that he understood exactly what I was going through and didn't take it lightly. As my husband had done previously, he told me that I needed to go see the doctor.

But I could never bring myself to go, mainly because I was concerned that a medical doctor would resort to putting me on medication, which I wanted no part of.

Daniel and I finally concluded that I needed to go see a specialist with whom I felt comfortable; namely, the doctor who had healed me of a liver ailment 15 years before. At that time my regular doctor and his team had run days of tests but couldn't diagnose my ailment. My husband and I had been dating about a year, and his mom had suggested that I go to see a holistic doctor that she knew. After only one visit with him and an altered diet using certain herbs for seasoning, I was completely cured of my liver condition, which has not ever revealed its tainted face again. So during my time of depression, I knew that I was well overdue for a visit to this holistic doctor.

That evening in our kitchen, I promised Daniel that I would call the doctor that next week (as it was a Friday evening when we were having this discussion). He said that according to his mom, the doctor will also do telephone consultations depending on your condition. I called on Tuesday, as Monday was a holiday in observance of Dr. Martin Luther King's birthday. The doctor told me that he couldn't do a proper diagnosis over the phone. Could I come in that same day? I did. After my two-hour visit, which consisted of what I consider muscle and mental therapy at his ocean-view office, I drove home with a new outlook on life.

The way I see it, depression is a welfare mentality because you are out of control of your life. Anytime something other than a positive mindset takes control of your life, this is a state of welfare. In order to combat this un-welcomed mentality, you must take action to regain control over your life. Following are the steps that helped me to start life anew with definition and purpose:

1. Exercise
2. Consult a therapist, chiropractor or holistic doctor and be honest in answering every question that you are asked. In other words, if you're not going to be truthful, don't bother with the visit.
3. Vocalize your feelings and tell the depression to get out!
4. Say to yourself daily: "I am happy. I am successful. I feel terrific!"
5. Take Brian Tracy's advice, and before going to bed each night, say to yourself, "In the morning I will wake up feeling terrific."
6. Meditate, envisioning the life that you desire.
7. Temporarily change your environment to one that will uplift you.
8. Surround yourself with positive people who feel good about themselves. (This is key!)
9. Read positive literature (books, magazines, etc.) and listen to positive, uplifting music. (Certain gospel artists work for me, such as Kirk Franklin, Yolanda Adams, and Trin-I-Tee: 5-7. Non-gospel artists that I love who provide tremendous upliftment are India.Arie, Heather Headley, Phil Collins and Mariah Carey.
10. Repeat steps 1-9.

If you follow this program, you may be well on your way to beating the depression, especially if you *believe* that you can overcome it. Don't ever think for a moment that depression cannot be vanquished. The moment you start thinking like this, you have already been defeated. Know that you are not a victim. You are a victorious survivor who deserves to live well and be well, and you can, as long as this is what you strongly believe. I know because I've been there and won the victory. So can you.

Side note: In hindsight I realized a few of the reasons that depression came into my life. But they could not be understood in the first 10 months of my semi-retired, launch-my-businesses-and-finish-my-book part of my life.

The first reason was that I was not living my life in line with that purpose which God had intended for me. As soon as I had not only realized my purpose, but also had the source of my depression revealed to me, the depression seemed to go away. But whenever I lost sight of that purpose, the depression re-introduced itself. This would happen every single time, prior to my visit with my holistic doctor.

So if you ever get depression as a visitor, be sure to take some time to think about your life and what you truly desire to do. Usually our deepest desires are in line with what God's intentions are for our lives. But sometimes we can get off track. Meditate daily and each night before you retire for the evening, ask God what your purpose is. You will be amazed at how soon you will receive an answer from God, and how much better you will start to feel, in such a short period of time.

Unless you've experienced depression yourself, you have no idea of the unfortunate power that it can have. If someone who was experiencing depression had explained to me that they suffered these same symptoms which I have described, and if I were ignorant about depression, I would suggest to them that they just think more positively and not allow such thoughts and behaviors to overtake them. Someone who responds in this manner to a human being that is depressed is unequivocally ignorant of depression and all of its impossibilities. I say "impossibilities" because this is exactly what depression attempts to persuade your mind -- that everything around you is impossible!

Depression is like a demonic virus that overtakes your body and drags you down to inaction. It causes you to feel defenseless, worthless, helpless, and useless. It is not to be taken lightly in any sense. Depression is something that can overcome a person and cause them to become the complete opposite of who they are accustomed to being. Their way of life is mostly turned upside down because there is a lack of desire to do anything! In short, depression is a living spirit that can overtake anyone, and it is best that we all understand and respect its terrible magnitude.

To the millions of people who suffer or have suffered from depression, I tell you now that I understand and empathize with you. Whatever you do, just don't ever allow it to prompt you to give up. Do not give it that power. Know that it is only temporary, regardless of how long you may have experienced its ugliness. When you're depressed, follow the suggestions that I have offered previously, and seek medical attention if necessary. As I mentioned in the introduction: know that this too shall pass. Believe this with all of your strength, and one day a celebration will be warranted.

It helps to know that you are not in this alone. According to The Health Center (www.thehealthcenter.info), depression is a common emotional disorder that affects about 7% of the population (which is equivalent to about 13-14 million people) in any given year. Also, the Center estimates that "7 million women in the United States are clinically depressed." In addition, it also goes on to say, "depression is the leading cause of disability in women", that "1 in 5 women will become clinically depressed over the course of her life." And that "Women are twice as likely as men to develop depression."

These statistics speak volumes about the prevalence of depression. The more that we educate ourselves as a population, the more able we can be at assisting those who are affected, possibly even helping ourselves. Again, depression is not to be taken lightly. If someone you know suffers from it, or even appears to be depressed, at minimum pray that it will not overcome them, and that they will rise triumphant, beating it in every aspect.

It wasn't until I realized all my reasons for being depressed, that I understood more fully how everything happens for a reason. Just as there are no accidents or mistakes, there was a definite reason or several reasons that I had to have this experience.

On Life and the Gift of Giving

My birth wasn't planned to say the least. In order for two parents to plan for a child, it is required that they first be together as a couple. My parents apparently missed this pre-requisite. They had previously dated in high school, and then were somehow re-connected many years later. However, these circumstances turned out to be more than ok because hey, had they planned for me, I may not have been the person I am today. So we will just say that God is *always* the ultimate Planner. Although I potentially was considered a mistake of two human beings known as my parents, it was God's Planned Parenthood and true intentions that brought me here.

It is therefore my duty to share with all those persons who exist in the world today, that regardless of the circumstances surrounding your birth, you were meant to grace us with your earthly presence. Even if you have been told repeatedly that you were a mistake, please know that in this life, there are no mistakes as long as God is involved. The universal God, who's the ultimate Creator, intended for us all to be here. There is a purpose (actually several purposes) for our existence and it is up to each one of us to realize our purpose, never becoming complacent with mediocrity.

Once we are living our lives on purpose, we will experience ultimate bliss, even during times of challenge and turmoil. When you live your life with purpose, everyday is seen as a blessing. And because we see it as such, we want to do nothing less than share our blessings with others, which is the primary reason that blessings are given to us in the first place. Blessings are not to be harbored, but spread out to bring joy into the lives of others. As long as we share our gifts, we will not be without additional gifts because this is how the purposeful life works.

If you were to close your hand and make a fist, how many diamond crystals could you place inside of that fist without opening it? None. But if you open your hand, you could fit an abundance of diamond crystals inside your hand. This is exactly how life works. As long as you keep your hand open to share your blessings with others, you allow more blessings to come in. But as soon as you close your hand into a tight fist, nothing can go in, and nothing comes out. Always remember this as you're going through life. Be open to share your blessings, and as you do this, more blessings will come into your life. As I have learned from Dr. Wayne Dyer, life is full of abundance. There are no shortages. The only shortages that exist are those that we create in our minds. See life in its abundant nature, and this is what you will get out of life: an abundance of your heart's desire.

You might want to re-visit the last paragraph of the prior section on depression where I discuss depression and living your life on purpose.

It has always been my desire to give to others, as this is one of the ultimate gifts in which God gives to us: the ability to share our talents with the world. I have always enjoyed writing, speaking, and just talking to others about various aspects of their lives, injecting hope and optimism at every possible turn.

One of the main reasons that I majored in psychology as an undergraduate was because I sincerely enjoyed helping people to improve their lives. Initially I had it all planned out. Roughly after my second or third year at California State University, Dominguez Hills (CSUDH), I had decided that I wanted to become a clinical psychologist. But after taking more psychology and sociology courses in my third and fourth year, I soon realized that I had a greater interest in children, and therefore wanted to become a child psychologist.

Then I became even more interested in child psychology after taking a class called "The Psychology of the Black Child" with a Professor Davis at CSUDH. There was (and apparently still is—maybe even more so now) a great deal of information on the disadvantages that black children face, even in the midst of a nation that is so ethnically diverse. During this class, I found it quite unfortunate that school-aged minority children, African-American children especially, were oftentimes stereotyped or prejudged prior to any completed assignments or interaction with their teachers. How is it that, as a teacher, you pre-determine the success or failure of any student before any form of student-teacher dialogue or written analysis is performed? Because of my personal and strong interest in the subject, I also read other books relative to the psychological aspects of raising and teaching minority children.

I find it both appropriate and necessary that all teachers, regardless of their location, become more intimately familiar with children (or people in general for that matter!) who are of a different cultural background than the one they are more accustomed to. I feel that this extra effort by teachers would assist in bridging the knowledge gap across cultures.

What a phenomenal teacher one must be who has traveled the world and spent quality time with people of various nations. Extravagant spending isn't necessary to do this. How wonderful it is that we can go around the world in a matter of a day or a week, by just picking up an in-depth book about any culture with which we are unfamiliar. If teachers would only travel like this, and submerge themselves culturally in other countries, they would surely be more inclined to understand the "problem" behaviors of a child, possibly even find a solution to that "problem."

This process, this change in teacher mentality, could change lives worldwide. Not only would the student's life become better served, but also the teacher would have a fulfillment beyond monetary gain, and society, as a whole would benefit from that child's enriched life. Instead of a life of turmoil and misunderstandings, the child would have the opportunity to find his or her own purpose. A child that is given a positive chance at life opens the door for many more children to share their gifts, dreams and talents with the world. As a nation, we can all do our part by utilizing care, concern, and optimism with every child. Although we don't know what the future holds, it sure looks a lot more promising when the kids who hold the key to it can feel good about who they are, and have a positive outlook on life.

This change will almost guarantee that the key continues to be passed on, so that more doors, which may have been previously locked, will now be opened.

About God

We have all spent time on disagreements or other disagreeable circumstances with family and friends. While those incidents did happen, I am more than sure that many, many joyous and favorable moments also happened as well. However, just from my experience within my own family, I know there's always that tendency of certain families to dwell on those very few unfavorable events, to the point that the good moments are completely ignored or forgotten.

In my family, for instance, whenever someone does something that isn't a good thing -- boy, does the word spread like wildfire! But if someone wins an award or does a nice deed, it probably only goes as far as the people who were in the room at the time, and maybe to one or two others. This is very unfortunate, and also something that I wanted to share with you.

While we are all human and unique individuals with our own opinions and preferences, we must always remember one thing: We should be free to disagree because of our honest differences of opinion, but we should not disagree to the point of creating disharmony, and maybe even saying things that we will eventually regret. Let's disagree, discuss it and be done with it. Let's not spend the next month harping on our disagreements. This is a waste of precious energy and time! Be free to disagree, but always allow harmony to remain, because life is too short to do otherwise.

Since I have been a Christian just about all of my life (since the age of 7), one of the realizations that I am blessed to know, is that God is everywhere at all times. He is with us even when we're doubting, or thinking that He has forgotten about us. He is always there. God knows each and every one of us very intimately. He knows our struggles and our disappointments. He has witnessed our upbringing, knowing how much we were loved or lacked being loved by our caretakers. He knows it all. So knowing all of this, He also knows who we are to this very day in our life, and the reason *why* we are the way that we are. And guess what? He still loves us the same!!

You see, it is not God who looks upon us unfavorably. As a Christian, I have also realized that the more Christian you become, the less judgmental you *should* become also, because it is not our place to judge anyone other than ourselves. We can only judge ourselves because, other than God, we are the only ones who know the most about our lives and ourselves. Honestly, we can only look upon our own lives and reflect upon what could have or should have been better with our lives. But we should not attempt to do this with the lives of other people.

I happen to know a Christian mother who dated a married man for over 15 years. When this was revealed to me, I often wondered how she could do this and live comfortably in her skin when she was a devout Christian. Secondly, how could she do this to another family? It bewilders me how some Christians can be concerned and overly dedicated to going to church every Sunday, and chastise others who don't frequent church as often, yet break one of the great commandments within the Christian faith. "Though shall not commit adultery." How is it that people can tell you that you shouldn't wear pants to church but believe in breaking up marital unions? I believe it clearly states "What God has put together, let no man (or woman) put asunder." Do people really believe in their religion, or is it just a routine?

This is one of the reasons why I've always believed that religion is not about going to church on Sunday, or what denomination you are, but mainly how you live your life every single day. Religion, in my opinion, is and always will be a way of life. This is where the word "religiously" comes in because it means what you do on a regular basis. When you do something *religiously*, you do it with conviction.

I was sourly disappointed once I found out that this Christian woman whom I had known and respected for quite some time, was dating a man who was married with a family. I did however now understand why certain people viewed marriage the way that they did, not necessarily being respectful of it and the vows that were taken before God. This is quite unfortunate, but something that I had to come to grips with. I also had to realize that although I don't agree with this woman's actions and behaviors, it is not my place to judge her.

I heard a minister say, "I can still love you, maybe even from a distance, and not agree with what you do. I love the person, but not their actions." After hearing this, it really helped me to know how to deal with certain people. None of us are perfect. We all have imperfections that we must cope with and work on, and I have come to this realization not only about others but also about myself. It is my hope that as we learn and grow, we become aware of our wrongdoings and make peace with those whom we have hurt in the process, and with ourselves.

Just as we were cradled in our mother's arms after first glimpsing light upon exiting our mother's womb, we will again be cradled as soon as we depart this physical life, only this time it will be upon God's bosom. He will cradle us in His arms and let us know that He was there the entire time, and He understands. We as humans here on Earth may not understand, but the one who matters most, our Loving and Just God, will understand. Let us always remember this.

I want each one of us to always remember that it is not our place to judge, because the minute that we do this, we have placed ourselves in God's shoes. And to place oneself in God's shoes is a mighty task to fulfill when you haven't a clue as to His shoe size. Stick to your own shoes, and God will allow you to run a magnificent race.

Until next time -- *think well and you will be well.*

Recommended Reading and Listening

For Spiritual Guidance:

The Power of Positive Thinking, by Dr. Norman Vincent Peale

The Power of Intention, by Dr. Wayne Dyer

The Seven Spiritual Laws of Success, by Deepak Chopra

The Psychology of Achievement, by Brian Tracy (cd series)

10 Secrets for Success and Inner Peace, by Dr. Wayne Dyer

The Prayer of Jabez, Breaking Through to the Blessed Life, by Bruce Wilkinson

Unstoppable, by Cynthia Kersey

How to Stop Worrying and Start Living, by Dale Carnegie

For Business Inspiration and Guidance:

True to yourself…leading a values-based business, by Mark Albion

Smart Women and Small Business, by Ginny Wilmerding

Ladies Who Launch…Embracing Entrepreneurship & Creativity As a Lifestyle, by Victoria Colligan & Beth Schoenfeldt with Amy Swift

The Breakthrough Company…How Everyday Companies Become Extraordinary Performers, by Keith R. McFarland

Appendix

In the wake of our current economic crisis, I would like to share information about a few resources for those in need of assistance. Whether you are facing foreclosure, a job loss, or financial strain, in addition to the inspirational mediums listed above, here are some viable resources to assist you during this financial crisis. I must however admit that because I am in the Greater Los Angeles area, most of the following resources are located in Southern California. But do not be discouraged. With a little time and research on the World-Wide-Web, I'm sure there are similar resources available in your area.

Please note that these are offered only as resources, and that the author does not endorse any particular organization nor does the author guarantee certain results by the reader contacting these entities. The author is also not responsible for any outcome, which may occur as a result of doing business with the resources listed. The reader is encouraged to do their own diligence and seek additional assistance outside of the resources listed when necessary, in order to make the best decision suited to their needs.

For homeowners and homebuyers in need of guidance and assistance:

NACA – Neighborhood Assistance Corporation of America (www.naca.com)

This is a non-profit community advocacy and Housing and Urban Development (HUD)-certified counseling agency. They provide step-by-step information and support in buying a first home, or renegotiating terms on a current unaffordable mortgage. For further and more detailed information please visit their website (listed above) or call 1-888-302-NACA. You may also email them at services@ naca.com for general information or requests for service regarding purchasing a home. For general information and inquiries regarding refinancing, please email them at refinance@naca.com; and to obtain general information and requests for services on predatory or unaffordable mortgages, email them at homesave@naca.com. NACA is especially beneficial for sub prime and low to moderate-income borrowers.

For loan modification programs that can either lower your mortgage payments or the principal balance on your mortgage, please first contact your lender directly. There are a few banks that have agreed to loan-modification programs for their borrowers, which are Citigroup, Bank of America, and JP Morgan Chase. Contrary to popular rhetoric, if homeowners wish to receive assistance with loan modification, it is not wise to voluntarily stop making mortgage payments. According to CNNMoney.com, this is ill advice that some homeowners have received; especially from unscrupulous companies attempting to solicit business from uninformed and financially stressed homeowners. If you are having trouble making mortgage payments, please contact your lender's loan modification department and explain to them your current situation.

If the loan-modification department for your lender is unwilling to work with you, don't give up hope. You may also call Hope Now at 888-995-HOPE or a HUD counselor at 800-569-4287. These hotlines offer counselors that may be able to assist you in the event your lender is unwilling to speak with you.

If you have suffered a job loss and are currently looking for new employment, most experts suggest that, above all, you should stay in contact with friends, family and colleagues, make new friends and network like crazy. Let those in your network know that you are currently looking for employment. The job market is highly competitive and as such, most jobs (80% of them, according to CNNMoney.com) are acquired through networking.

Also, be sure to post your resume online, and utilize social networking sites such as Facebook (www.facebook.com), Twitter (www.twitter.com) and Linked-In (www.linkedin.com). There are many different online job sites, so be sure to focus on those containing postings for your industry. Here are some sites to get you started:

www.careerbuilder.com - This site features jobs offered nationwide in various industries and across varying job levels.

www.careerladder.com - Jobsite for professionals seeking positions with salary offerings over $100k.

www.efinancialcareers.com - Site for those seeking careers in the financial industry.

www.selectleaders.com - Job search site for real estate jobs.

www.indeed.com - Job search site for a variety of industries.

www.usajobs.gov - The official site for US government jobs.

Last but not least -- it is imperative to stay optimistic during these turbulent times, so remember to spend your time in the company of positive people. This simple and small concept could make a tremendous positive impact on your life and outlook. Additionally, it is also vitally important to remain mentally optimistic. Counter those negative thought patterns with a verbal positive thought. As we know – and this has been the constant theme of my book – our thoughts have amazing power, so focus your energy on that which you want to be true.

****

Acknowledgments

There were quite a few people who were instrumental in assisting me to see this book through to fruition.

To my husband and life-long friend, Daniel:

I know that this has been a long time coming, and I thank you, thank you, thank you, for understanding during all of the sleepless nights I caused you, when I had those brainstorming moments between 2 and 5 a.m. Thank you for your continued support and encouragement, even during the midst of chaos. Although sometimes we faced quite the challenge, we knew, as long as we believed it to be so, that we would make it successfully through.

To my daughter Neemah:

You give me purpose beyond words (and not just because this is the meaning behind your name!). Thank you so much for your continued inspiration and motivation. You are one of the main reasons that I strive to be at my best in all that I do, because there's no way that I can expect you to do so if I'm not providing the example.

Continue in your writing and all of your endeavors. As long as you view them as your gifts to the World, we all will be enriched.

To my unofficial pre-publishing, reading committee: Rashida Coleman, Carolyn Drayton, Katrina Hopwood, Patricia Isom, Myia Odom-Bey, Melanie Reed, and Donna Shaw. Thanks so much to each of you for your words of encouragement and constructive input upon reading my initial submissions. Because of your enthusiasm, all of you were quite instrumental in helping me get this project completed in a timely manner. Your support is what kept me going with the reassurance that this book was definitely worthwhile. Thanks a million times over.

To my extended family, friends, colleagues, teachers and associates, thanks to each of you for continuously encouraging, supporting and believing in me, and for providing some of the stimuli to make this book not only possible, but a must!